# STRANGERS TO
# SUPERFANS

## A Marketing Guide to the Reader Journey

David Gaughran was born in Ireland but now lives in a quaint little fishing village in Portugal, although this doesn't seem to have increased the time he spends outside. He writes historical fiction and science fiction under another name, has helped tens of thousands of authors publish their work and build a career for themselves through his workshops, blog, and writers' books—*Let's Get Digital, Strangers to Superfans, Amazon Decoded, BookBub Ads Expert*, and *Following*—and has also created giant marketing campaigns for some of the biggest self-publishers on the planet. Visit David Gaughran.com to get yourself a free book.

"David Gaughran knows more about book marketing than anyone on the planet, always on the cutting edge of what's working in a market that is constantly changing. Skip his wisdom at your peril."
—*USA Today* bestselling author Ernest Dempsey

**Praise for *Let's Get Digital:***
***How To Self-Publish, And Why You Should***

"*Let's Get Digital* is a must read for anyone considering self-publishing."

—JA Konrath, bestselling author of
*Trapped*, *Origin*, and *Whiskey Sour*

"It should be the starting point for anyone considering self-publishing today. Required reading for any indie author."

—Sharon Rosen, *Pixel of Ink*

ISBN-13: 978-91-87109-30-0

Editor: Tammi Labrecque
Cover: Alexios Saskalidis, 187Designz

**DavidGaughran.com**

Updated paperback edition published August 2020

A **MARKETING GUIDE**
TO THE READER JOURNEY

# STRANGERS TO
# SUPERFANS

# DAVID GAUGHRAN

# CONTENTS

*To Phoenix,*
*for dragging me out of the ditch.*

# Introduction

We've all walked similar paths. I know from speaking with lots of writers, on forums and at conferences and in workshops, that most of us started out thinking we had a discoverability problem. *The book is good*, we told ourselves, *I just need to reach the right people and it will take off.* And that was kind of true in 2010 or 2011. Professional presentation and a hooky blurb, combined with a price firmly in impulse buy territory, was often enough to get sales moving.

By 2013, the Kindle Store had grown well beyond one million titles, and the challenge became one of visibility. I published a book called *Let's Get Visible: How To Get Noticed And Sell More Books*, which broke down how the Kindle Store worked and why authors should tweak their marketing to take advantage of how the various algorithms functioned—like spreading launch juice over several days rather than hitting everything at once. Or, to be more accurate, I documented the efforts of some very successful self-publishers who had cracked the Amazon code.

And that approach—which you might call Visibility Marketing—worked very well for a few years and helped a few people step up to the next level. In fact, the book was popular enough that I still get regular requests to bring out a new edition. Eventually, after four years, I agreed it was time. But when I began, I realized the game had shifted completely. Instead of one million books in the Kindle Store, there were now eight million. The average self-publisher was much savvier and had more titles out, with generally slicker presentation. Fortunes had been made by some, and many were plowing that back into ever-more-sophisticated marketing plans.

The opportunities to reach new eyeballs had grown, but not at the same pace as the huge uptick in content. Visibility challenges had become visibility chokepoints. Even when authors did manage to get readers to their Amazon product page, there were a whole bunch of noisy distractions tempting them away from the Buy button.

And all of that was only the beginning of the challenges facing today's self-publishers. It was clear that what was needed was a fresh approach, a new paradigm.

This book will teach you how to look at marketing in a new way, from the perspective of the people most critical to your business: your readers. It will teach you how to identify your Ideal Readers, and explain the five different stages of The Reader Journey from strangers to superfans. You will learn how to optimize each stage and lose as few of these precious people as possible along the way.

Not only that, it will give you a new, more powerful, and efficient way to manage your backlist. It will pinpoint the flaws in your marketing and help you revitalize sales on books that have fallen away. And it will teach you how to launch the right way, from the start, so you don't go running off in the wrong direction, making expensive mistakes and creating trouble for tomorrow.

Let me explain quickly how this book is structured, because it starts off quite conceptual, and you might worry that there will be no practical application. Fear not! We'll get our hands dirty after we map out the territory.

**Part I** has the fabulously grandiose title of *A New Paradigm—The Reader Journey*. It covers how marketing has changed and how the latest approaches translate very well into the world of books. It explains the importance of granular targeting and helps you identify your Ideal Reader.

**Part II** outlines the five states that readers pass through on their Reader Journey from strangers to superfans: Discovery, Visibility, Consideration, Purchase, and Advocacy. Then it dives right into the action, rooting out blockages like discoverability myths, visibility chokepoints, and the distraction crisis playing out on our Amazon product pages.

**Part III** tackles the escalating problem of conversion by showing you how to optimize each stage of The Reader Journey, from getting discovered to converting browsers into buyers and turning DNFs into OMGs.

**Part IV** unveils The Failure Matrix, which is such a cool name I almost used it as the title for this book. It's also a system for helping you identify blockages in your own Reader Journey, so you can manage backlist efficiently and spend more of your time and energy on writing, instead of endlessly puzzling over non-performing titles, wondering what to fix. When we're finished, you'll be able to tell a Visibility Fail from a Consideration Fail, and you'll know exactly where to send the nanobots. You'll also know in what order to accomplish these tasks (and understand why that's important).

**Part V** draws everything together and teaches you how to renovate every aspect of a book, series, or entire catalog at once, and why it's important to work backwards and deal with the product and presentation before the promotion.

And to help you apply all the knowledge you will learn in this book, I've assembled a collection of bonus resources, which are exclusive to readers of this book; this will also serve as a handy repository for all the links, tools, and services mentioned here, as well as somewhere you can ask questions. Access this Resources page on a private part of my website—*DavidGaughran.com/ SuperfansResources*. No need to bookmark that link now; I will repeat it throughout.

One last thing: don't be overwhelmed. Selling books is more complicated today but the tools we have at our disposal are much more sophisticated and the readers are out there in greater numbers than ever. The bar has been raised. It's time for us to do the same, and refocus on readers.

*Strangers to Superfans: A Marketing Guide to The Reader Journey* will show you how.

# PART I

## A NEW PARADIGM— THE READER JOURNEY

Increased competition means that the challenges facing self-publishers have grown much more complex. Luckily, there is a new marketing paradigm that can help us understand why some readers buy our books when others don't. I call it "The Reader Journey." And the protagonist of this story is someone you need to understand a little deeper: your Ideal Reader.

# 1: The New Marketing

Marketing has changed and publishing has fallen behind, once again. While our industry has never really been on the cutting edge, a recent shift in the wider marketing world completely passed us by.

My own professional background is in tech and marketing, and I decided to refresh my skill-set a little while ago. I started off getting AdWords certified again. It's not a great platform for selling books, but it is still a good grounding in the basic principles of digital marketing and was an easy way for me to shake the cobwebs loose. From there, I delved into content marketing and inbound marketing—in some cases it was just updated jargon and tools, but there were some interesting new concepts too. One idea that stood out was that of "The Buyer Journey"—and I could immediately see how well it would translate into the world of books and readers and, lately, algorithms.

The basic concept was straightforward, and it was a mindset shift more than anything, away from the idea of sales funnels. Traditionally, businesses looked at marketing from the perspective of *their* company and the effect marketing has on *their* sales (sometimes forgetting about *their* customers in the process). The Buyer Journey didn't allow you to do that. It was a POV shift to the customer, training you to view all your products and marketing messages from the buyer perspective.

But before all this gets too abstract, let's jump over to the world of books and start applying these concepts in tangible, familiar forms.

## Translating the Buyer Journey

Have you read *On Writing* by Stephen King? Whether you're a fan of his fiction or not, it's an interesting book, the first I read that spoke about writing in a matter-of-fact way without leaning on some faux-mystical babble. King talked about writing as a craft, rather than an art, which helped me immensely—and still does. (I think it's both a craft *and* an art, but internally classifying it as the former gives me a better work ethic, quite frankly.)

Anyway, the concept in that book that I want to highlight was that of the Ideal Reader. For Stephen King, his wife Tabitha is his Ideal Reader—the person he envisages when writing his stories, the person his books are truly meant for. Thinking about his Ideal Reader when working on a novel ensures he doesn't go far wrong.

Lots of us have adopted this approach in one form or another. We often think about our own work as being attractive to one set of readers, but perhaps not to another, even within specific genres and niches—the "spice" levels in Romance being a simple and obvious example.

Literary tastes are incredibly balkanized. Any given SF/F junkie might dig space battles and adore reading about dragons but despise the two together. Or they might think your space fantasy featuring intergalactic dragons breathing positronic rays that create a temporal distortion field is the coolest thing ever. Some police procedural devotees might roll their eyes at yet another boozy workaholic detective with problems at home, yet others might delight in your fresh and subversive take on this most reliable of tropes. We can all think of similar examples because most readers' tastes are quite refined, in all genres.

And thank heavens for that! Otherwise it would be like Hollywood and there would be a handful of story studios cornering the market. The kind of operation James Patterson is running would be the rule, rather than the exception. Which is fine if your name is James Patterson...

Your Ideal Reader doesn't need to be your own spouse (or Stephen King's for that matter). In fact, it doesn't need to be a specific person in the real world. It's often an idealized person, a composite with certain aggregate traits from your readership. And it doesn't necessarily need to be too specific, at least to begin with. For example, I know that my Ideal Reader is a college-educated woman between the age of 35 and 54 who owns her own home. And it's her shoes I need to put myself in, to judge the effectiveness of my marketing efforts.

I need to imagine how she feels when she sees a BookBub email containing my cover. I have to figure out why she hesitated before clicking the Buy button. I must try to determine why she liked my book enough to finish it, but not sufficiently to recommend it. And it's truly important to understand why she didn't buy the next book. The answers to all of those questions are different in one sense—and we'll go through all of them and lots more in turn—but they all spring from one fatal flaw.

I didn't know her well enough.

# 2: Defining Your Ideal Reader

Imagine simply plonking a house down on a random piece of land, without surveying the ground or laying any foundations. And while the Boomers are horrified by that example, let's do a Take 2 for the Millennials: imagine applying for an internship without checking if there was an actual, real path to a paying job that wouldn't make you cry-eat your hair on the subway home. My point is that research is important. And while we're getting updates from Captain Obvious: preparation is crucial.

We're in a bit of a bind these days. There are immensely powerful tools at our disposal, but hitting that critical mass of readers that most of us are chasing also requires some investment. As such, we need to be absolutely sure we're pointed in the right direction before we go charging into battle.

Which means you'd better know your Ideal Reader, for on her mighty shoulders rests your entire marketing edifice. And if you place that burden on the wrong pair of shoulders, it will all come crumbling down and your

FAKE NEWS Ideal Reader will slowly deteriorate in the desert like some bargain store Ozymandias, forgotten to all but extreme Breaking Bad nerds.

To avoid this awful fate, you must:

1.  Determine who your Ideal Reader is;
2.  Find out where she likes to hang out;
3.  Capture her for your personal cloning scientist Igor Von Facebook.

Ahem.

Let's start at the top. Perhaps you have some idea who your Ideal Reader is. Possibly you even know *exactly* who he or she is. Or maybe you don't know at all.

We'll start with the latter assumption, as running through the process could help anyone from the other camps define their Ideal Reader a little more exactly. Besides, you may need to identify several different Ideal Readers to cover your entire target readership—which can be true even for those who write in strictly one niche.

You might have noticed me saying before that my Ideal Reader is "a college educated woman between the age of 35 and 54 who owns her own home." Aside from instinctively knowing that my readers are intelligent, cosmopolitan types with impeccable taste, how did I figure this out? Facebook told me. Facebook gives you a demographic breakdown of who has liked your page: their age, gender, marital status, household income, other interests, and so on. There is even more detailed information in the "Audience Insights" section of Facebook. You really should take a gander, as it allows you to access (aggregate, anonymized) information on who has Liked your Page *and* lets you compare it to other, similar Pages.

Even more valuable is something long-rumored: Amazon opening up the treasure trove of reader data that is Goodreads. At the moment, these insights are only available to Amazon Publishing authors, but Amazon has been considering opening this up to KDP authors for some time—things like aggregate demographics on who has shelved our books in Goodreads. This would be the motherlode, obviously, but until that happy day we'll have to make do with other sources.

Talking to readers is an excellent start. I hope that you all include contact information in your books so readers can reach out to you, and that you try to personally respond to any fan mail in a reasonable timeframe. Moving beyond simple platitudes might allow you to learn a little more about your readership. Even better is building an email relationship with as many of your readers as possible via your mailing list, something I'll talk about more later in this book. Doing the same via a Facebook Page allows a more accurate collection of demographics and preferences, and analyzing the results of any advertising you do will give you further valuable data.

You don't need to do any advertising or analysis to get some of the best data out there, though; simply look at your Author Page on Amazon, as well as the product pages for each of your individual books. On your Author Page, underneath your mugshot and bio, you'll see a section titled "Customers Also Bought Items By." This clunky phrase does more than just force me to end a sentence with a preposition; it also tells you what other authors your readers enjoy—which is incredibly valuable information when it comes to advertising on Facebook and BookBub and Amazon, but also helps round out the picture you are beginning to form of your Ideal Reader.

If you write in more than one niche, this data might only give you a partial picture, and you'll get much more joy from drilling down into the Also Boughts on each of your book's product pages. Note the authors and titles that keep popping up—again very handy data for advertising, but also to help you get to know your Ideal Reader that little bit better.

Through all of these things—conversations with readers; Audience Insights on Facebook; results from Amazon, BookBub, and Facebook Ads; authors and titles that keep showing up in your Also Boughts on Amazon—you should start getting a better picture of who your Ideal Reader is, what they like, and what they very much don't. These are the only people you want to target, which means fighting against your artistic instincts, and possibly divesting yourself of some myths about marketing too.

# 3: The Importance of Granular Targeting

I began working in digital marketing fifteen years ago. A lot has changed, but one thing has remained constant: the critical importance of granular targeting. This was a completely new paradigm in the world of advertising. The old model, which dominated until the beginning of the 21$^{st}$ century, was the broadcast approach: get that message out to everyone. Blast it out in all directions. If the signal is strong enough, the right people will hear it.

This approach leads to disaster online, which is all about being discriminating, zooming in, finding your core audience (i.e. your Ideal Readers), and targeting them. Exclusively. Digital advertising is the cheapest and most effective way to reach customers… if your targeting is solid. If you are aiming at the wrong people, it can be the biggest waste of money.

On top of that, most digital advertising platforms actively reward good targeting through delivering cheaper clicks or free exposure for well targeted ads. Bad targeting just creates a hole in your budget, a dent in your sales, and a huge opportunity for a savvy competitor. Good targeting can generate immediate returns and can even outmaneuver a bigger player with deeper pockets, if you are smart about it.

An example: If I advertise one of my historical novels to the general Historical Fiction audience on BookBub, the take-up will be relatively small. I might see a click-through rate (CTR) of 0.5%-1% with that broad, general audience, even when advertising a 99¢ deal. Clicks can cost as much as $2 each with that kind of CTR, which is crazy. Given that I'm only earning 35¢ on each one of those 99¢ sales, this is a great way to go broke fast.

However, if I think about the college-educated home-owning women who makes up the core of my historical readership, I might suspect that they also like reading Patrick O'Brian. And as soon as I target his readers instead of the general Historical Fiction audience, my click-through rate jumps to 3.5%-4% on that same ad. That means clicks are now costing 25¢ or less and starting to look more viable, particularly if this is the first book in a series with good sell-through. One simple little tweak—one added level of granularity to the targeting—dropped costs by almost 90%.

Similarly, there are over two billion different adults you can target on Facebook, but you are far better off drilling right down to the subset of readers who are most likely to purchase. There might be only 10,000 such people when you drill down, but limiting your audience like this is infinitely better than advertising broadly. Our natural inclination as artists is to be read by as many people as possible, but we must fight against that instinct when it comes to online advertising. We need to target the right people exclusively, otherwise it gets expensive fast and you will run out of money very quickly. And there will be none coming back in via book sales, either.

We'll return to advertising later; I merely mention these examples now to underline the importance of targeting, but if you do want to delve into this topic further, check the articles recommended on the Resources page for this book at *DavidGaughran.com/SuperfansResources*. Keep in mind that if you don't know who your Ideal Reader is, or have drawn an inexact picture of them, you will be targeting the wrong people.

# 4: Buyer Personas & The Stages of Selling

Marketers in the wider world have been applying insights from The Buyer Journey approach for several years now. They take a huge amount of care when constructing what they call "Buyer Personas."

Buyer Personas are semi-fictional, in the sense that they are archetypes based on market research and real data about existing customers. Marketers will construct several Buyer Personas to cover their entire target market. They delve into demographics, behavior, motivations, and goals, in as much detail as possible, and allow these insights to guide product development as well as marketing.

If you are an insurance company looking to pitch your new product line of pet insurance products, knowing that one of your key Buyer Personas is a soccer mom with two kids and a part-time job is incredibly important. The ad you might set up targeting people like her would be very different than one to remind seniors that it's a good idea to have coverage for end-of-life costs.

Similarly, your Buyer Personas might indicate a gap in your offerings. Perhaps you provide travel insurance that's mostly suitable for short trips, and doesn't cover various higher-risk activities like waterskiing and bungee jumping, but you notice that a significant portion of your customer base are college students, going on extended trips around Asia and engaging in various proscribed activities, who are forced to go to a competitor, or risk traveling without insurance—a market you could easily cover with a higher-premium product.

Know your audience, in other words. And at this stage my internal klaxon is sounding, reminding me to get bookish.

This process can be a little like filling out one of those character sheets that some authors swear by to get a better picture of their hero. Height, weight, eye color, speech affectations, education level, and marital status— but also favorite TV show, most used social media network, political persuasion, and whether they enjoy Brussels sprouts. Like with plotting and outlining, those exercises can be useful… if your mind works that way. Others might prefer to trust the bloodhound instincts of their gut, giving it little sniffs of reader-meat, then letting it loose in the forest to see what it uncovers.

You know your own damn self.

Take all the info that's out there about your audience. Ponder it. Form an idea of who you are writing for, what they like, what turns them off, where they hang out—online, I mean; don't actually stalk people. Fill out one of those character sheets for your Ideal Reader if it helps you get a better sense of them, or check the suggestions on the Resources page for this book at *DavidGaughran.com/SuperfansResources* if you really want to go deep on this. And don't worry if you hit a few blanks along the way. You can revisit this. I do that all the time! A vague idea of who your Ideal Reader is will suffice for now. It can be honed later.

## The Stages of Selling

I was several months into querying agents when I had an insight—not that I should self-publish; that one would come a few (hundred) rejections later. What I realized is that a book must be sold several times before it makes it into a reader's hands. Even if an agent is bowled over by your query letter and your manuscript, she must sell it to an editor at a publishing house. If the editor acquires your book, they must sell it internally to the sales and marketing teams, convincing them that the book is worth backing. Then the sales teams must sell it to the buyers for the bookstores. The employees of the bookstores must then attempt to make the final sale, to the reader, who may or may not purchase after all that.

But there are several other points beforehand where any book could fail to be sold.

The mistake I made, as beginning writers often do, was to focus exclusively on that first "sale." I focused on learning how to write the perfect query letter instead of writing the next book or working on my craft.

It's the same with The Reader Journey. We often focus on the first stage—Discovery—to the expense of everything else. But there are five stages our Ideal Reader passes through on the journey from stranger to superfan. Each stage demands our attention, because each represents a potential failure point where we could lose precious readers. In fact, I will argue later that each stage represents an escalating challenge of conversion, one which needs to be optimized in very different ways.

Let's take a look at The Reader Journey:

1. **Discovery.** This is when your Ideal Reader has never heard of you, seen one of your covers, or encountered your books.
2. **Visibility.** Your Ideal Reader is somewhat aware of you. Maybe they saw you in BookBub or in someone else's Also Boughts.
3. **Consideration.** Your Ideal Reader is in the building! I mean, they are on your product page on Amazon or elsewhere and contemplating hitting that Buy button.

4. **Purchase.** They bought it! You are now 35¢-$3.49 richer. But will they like it?
5. **Advocacy.** Holy crap, they are telling people on Twitter to read your book, linking to your Amazon listing where they left a five-star review, and promoting you in meatspace too.

How did this happen? How can you make it happen more often? In short, we're going to optimize conversion at every point, because each stage is another hurdle which your Ideal Reader may not clear. First, let's break down each stage in detail, and gain a deeper understanding of what can prevent our Ideal Readers from becoming superfans.

# PART II

## READER ROADBLOCKS

In this section, we'll detail the five stages our Ideal Readers pass through on their journey from strangers to superfans: Discovery, Visibility, Consideration, Purchase, and Advocacy. We'll also show the very different things that can go wrong at each stage, and the way writers always make the mistake of focusing on one stage exclusively and apply Discovery solutions to different classes of problem, or think the Reader Journey ends with a purchase. Crap, that's a lot of stuff. Brace yourselves!

# 5: The Discoverability Myth

There is nothing more magical than discovering a great book; we forget this. We can sometimes think of advertising and promotion as a form of trickery, overcoming reader resistance to our work. But if we are marketing correctly, all we are doing is helping readers discover books that *we already know* they will love. Indie bookstores can be great at this, pressing a book into your hands *knowing* you will adore it. Friends are even better; with a history of knowing your tastes, they can recommend anything with confidence.

And yet.

Recommendations can miss the mark, no matter how well informed the recommender. Taste ·is resolutely individual. This simple fact is the best and worst thing about publishing. It creates the ridiculous diversity of opinion that supports an infinity of voices, but also makes it incredibly difficult to identify the exact readers who like your work, resulting in what is often a very hit-and-miss approach for both readers and authors. A lot of frogs tend to be kissed.

Flipping this around, there are millions of books you will never read. You might discover new authors in all sorts of ways, and have very eclectic tastes, but the simple fact is that there are many times more stories that you will never encounter in any form, at any time, even if you dedicate the rest of your life to reading. This has ramifications for author-you. Even if you are writing the type of book that your Ideal Readers love, you start off completely unknown to them. Which is great! It means that all your books are *new to them* no matter when they were published.

Writers tie themselves into knots over the Discovery stage, and there is a real danger of missing the magic here. As I will counsel you repeatedly in this book, you must put yourself in the shoes of your Ideal Reader. And maybe imagine Morgan Freeman saying this instead of me.

"There are millions of books you will never read…"

I don't know about you, but I find that both exciting and scary. There are so many books, yet people manage to find new ones every day. It's like reverse-conception, a reader hurtling towards millions of book-eggs.

Okay, it's not like that at all. My point is, part of the magic of discovery revolves around this crazy oversupply of books and weirdly granular tastes. "I like Steampunk murder mysteries only if the detective is a shifter but there better be absolutely no goddamn vampires" is the kind of amusingly specific thing we hear all the time from readers. Taste is resolutely individual. There are loads of things we could read, many of which would be *okay I guess*. But finding something we truly love… that often seems kind of miraculous.

What put that individual book into our hands at that exact moment might be a little more tangible though. Perhaps it was a Christmas gift. A recommendation from a colleague. Maybe the cover jumped out at you on Amazon when you were looking for something else. The possibilities are endless, but they all describe a reader who was a stranger to the author—a person completely unaware of that writer's work, someone who had never heard their name or seen one of their covers.

Most readers, in other words.

This is the first stage of the Reader Journey: Discovery. But it's not the last. Discovery is the easiest problem to solve, but also the easiest to screw up. Anyone can buy traffic, but if you don't target the right readers, everything that you build on those foundations is going to be wobbly. Yet we screw it up here all the time. We always do it in the same way too: forgetting ourselves. Think how particular you are in your own tastes. Now consider how indiscriminate you can be with targeting. A common mistake is to advertise in a suboptimal venue or target a group slightly outside your niche, thinking you can convince them to give you a try.

We always think it's a Discovery problem, but some-times the worst solution is more oxygen. Yet that's always what we reach for. An ad doesn't work, and we turn up the juice, or just try another venue. Or a slightly tweaked graphic. Or fiddle with the targeting. We can be very slow to check if the problem is elsewhere. Meanwhile we are burning through our marketing budget.

It's a kind of madness, but a perfectly understandable one. It's easy to lose your bearings when your books are deep in the telephone rankings, no reviews are coming in, nothing is happening on social media, and no readers are talking about your work. This is your new release, and it just *bombed*.

Gulp.

But the moment passes, and determination kicks in. You decide on a plan, resolving to blow this sucker up. Throw an internet's worth of traffic at her. Burn through some money until she has lift-off. Speculate to accumu-late, right? And then the next day you try to justify the mediocre sales reports. "I Thought They Would Buy Book 5" will be chiseled into your gravestone, home to moss and dog pee and nobody's tears.

- We obsess about the Discovery stage at the expense of *even noticing* other challenges.
- We think solving a Discovery problem will make any book sell (and we're wrong).
- We waste money on Discovery solutions when we have issues at different stages.

Some history: when ebooks first exploded between late 2010 and early 2012, a bunch of publishing consultants began doing the rounds, peddling the theory that there was a "discoverability problem" with e-books, particularly with stores like Amazon. It was quite strange for this theory to suddenly surface when it never reared its head during the initial switch to online purchasing. Then I realized who the audience was: publishing companies.

When publishers began parroting these concerns, I knew what they really meant. There wasn't a discoverability problem in ebookstores; the real problem was that readers were discovering books published by other people: self-publishers and small publishers and other non-traditional actors that had been sidelined in a print world but were grabbing a bigger piece of the pie now that the market had opened up.

The so-called discoverability problem was always nonsense, but it planted firm roots at the traditional end of the industry because it told people what they wanted to hear—much in the same way the myth about a flattening or declining ebook market is repeated and retweeted gleefully today no matter what the data actually says.

The truth is that readers have little problem discovering books; in fact, many Kindle owners find it much easier to find something they enjoy now that prices are much more competitive, and they can order from millions of titles that are delivered instantly without them having to leave home. Also, they shop at a store where the recommendations are predominantly influenced by what they browse for and purchase and read, rather than what the big publisher or store manager or oh-so-important critic has deemed the "book of the month."

My own experience is reflective of this. The act of visiting a bricks-and-mortar bookstore, wandering the aisles to see what you serendipitously discover, might be more magical, but despite that, I spend a lot more time browsing online bookstores now. I purchase more books, I can *afford* more books, and, thanks to things like recommendation algorithms and free sampling, I also rarely hit a dud these days.

And when I do, I'm not stuck with it. There's a library of hundreds of books at my fingertips and I can order new titles whenever I want. My problem isn't finding books—quite the opposite. The real issue is finding enough time to read everything.

As an author, the challenge at the Discovery stage is not, as many think, cutting through the noise. A Discovery problem is actually the easiest to solve, because anyone can buy traffic. However, a Discovery problem is also the easiest to solve *incorrectly*, because people often purchase the *wrong* traffic.

We'll talk about how to solve all these problems more deeply in subsequent chapters, but let me just say this for now: if you aim at the wrong readers, and they buy your book, then Amazon's system will have an incorrect picture of who might like your books—often reflected in the wrong Also Boughts appearing on your product page on Amazon. Then every time you manage to get some visibility, Amazon will begin recommending your book via email, or on site… to the wrong people. This cycle can be hard to break out of, and you must do your utmost to avoid it.

It might be relatively straightforward to solve Discovery issues, but you still must do so with care and with one eye on your targeting at all times—exclusively aiming for your Ideal Readers wherever possible.

# 6: Visibility Chokepoints

You know when someone recommends a book you were interested in but subsequently forgot about? "Oh, I've been meaning to check that out," you might respond, before one-clicking it onto your device, thankful for the reminder.

Of course, these days your helpful friend doesn't need to be an actual meatbag; it can be BookBub or Facebook or Amazon, or the *New York Times*, I guess. At any given point as a reader, there will be a variety of books on your radar, so to speak, only some of which you might be directly conscious of, as they lie in wait like narrative landmines.

Readers are tangentially aware of you at the Visibility Stage. They might spot you in the Also Boughts of a more popular book. They may run their eyes over your cover in the BookBub Featured Deals email, as if it were a *barely there* swimsuit on a vacuous celebrity. Or they may bounce off your ad text on Facebook, cold to your caffeine-soaked hype. But you're on their radar. You have somehow crawled out of the great primordial soup of wordsmithery and introduced yourself to their consciousness. In other words: you exist.

But enough about you and your problems! Let's refocus on the true protagonist in this story: the reader. At this stage of The Reader Journey, your Ideal Reader is tangentially aware of you, or has just encountered your books for the first time. Maybe they saw your cover in Amazon Search when hunting for books on managing personal finances. Or perhaps they were checking out the bestselling book in that category when your bright cover and snappy title caught their eye.

This is the Visibility Stage. Maximizing visibility at Amazon is a key goal. While authors would like to be visible everywhere, we tend to focus on Amazon for three key reasons. First, it's the biggest store with the most customers, so the return on any effort to become more visible is generally greater. Second, we understand how Amazon works, to a certain extent; we know how to optimize promotions to increase visibility at Amazon, while retailers like Apple Books and Nook are much more of a black box. Third, Amazon is the retailer that provides us with the most level playing field, making the lion's share of high-visibility spots up for grabs to any author or publisher who performs well enough organically with readers, rather than auctioning that real estate off to the highest bidder (i.e. big publishers) like many other retailers do—a corollary of how it works in the world of print.

Speaking more generally, in case you're wondering, we also tend to focus on being visible at online retailers, rather than in any other location, as reducing the amount of time and space between the reader encountering your cover and being able to click the Buy button greatly increases conversion.

This tactic of working the algorithms and maximizing visibility on Amazon was pretty groundbreaking in 2013 and is still very useful. But it's no longer enough. While the market has grown considerably since then, and while the tools we have for reaching readers are much more sophisticated, the number of titles has grown exponentially. More importantly, the number of spots for visibility on Amazon has not kept pace with this growth at all.

There is an outsized focus on the raw number of titles in the Kindle Store—partly due to the discoverability myth I spoke about in the last chapter. A lot of handwringing accompanied the news that the number of titles had passed four million, or five million, or six million. It's eight million now, and I'm sure it will be ten million soon enough, and the volume on this will get turned all the way up. Which is very interesting to me, because nobody noticed when the number of print titles hit ten million, or fifteen million, itself a mere fraction of the total available outside of Amazon and in secondhand bookstores and libraries.

We also need perspective in another way. A third of those eight million titles have no rank on Amazon, meaning they have never sold a copy, not even to themselves for testing. The author or publisher just slapped the book up and obviously has done little or nothing to market it. Many other books are ranked north of two million in the rankings, not having sold a single copy for months and months.

These books aren't providing any meaningful competition for visibility spots.

Here's a much more important number: 100. That's the number of spots in the Amazon Top 100, as you might have surmised. Another one: 13,000. That's roughly the number of categories and subcategories in the Kindle Store, each with their own Best Seller list, meaning there are over one million chart positions you could potentially feature in. Once you factor in Top Rated lists and Hot New Releases lists and Movers & Shakers, and then the 15,000+ categories and subcategories for print books, all with their own charts, the number of total potential visibility spots climbs well into the millions.

And that's just the beginning. There are Also

Boughts on many of those eight million titles and sponsored results on most of them, there are search results, and there are recommendations that appear in other places—such as after a reader purchases a book. As a result, the total number of opportunities for visibility on Amazon dwarfs the number of titles.

Of course, not all visibility is equal; it's much more important to appear in the Top 100 of the Kindle Store than it is to appear in the Top 100 of the Latin American Historical Fiction chart, which can't even muster up more than five titles for its Hot New Releases chart (alas). And it matters a lot more being the first Also Bought in a hot book in your niche than one ranked way out in the millions, no matter how good it might be.

These are the breaks.

# 7: Consideration Distraction

Your Ideal Reader is on your product page—sound the Horn of Impending Victory! This rare specimen got there via a Facebook ad he dutifully clicked on, and is *at this very moment* weighing up a purchase. He's not one of the readers who was immediately sold by the cover or hooked by the blurb. Our prospective reader likes the sound of the book but is searching for something to tip him over the edge and compel him to purchase: he's scanning the reviews, skimming your carefully chosen blurb quotes. After an interminable period of prevarication, he finally clicks the Buy button. Phew.

Most readers don't do this. Instead, they click away elsewhere, deciding the book isn't for them or distracted by something temporarily more alluring, or bread burning in the toaster, perhaps. The simplicity of digital publishing is a double-edged sword. It's great to upload to five stores and cover 99% of the market, but that obviously means they have all the power. I have minimal input into how my own books are presented to readers on Amazon—or anywhere else for that matter. As a result, ads for other books have slowly taken over our listings.

At this point, distraction is the last thing we need readers to be subjected to. We have spent time and money and energy getting discovered, ensured our audience has navigated a variety of visibility chokepoints, and finally got our Ideal Reader onto our product page— and now they're faced with a wall of ads for books. *Other* books, i.e. not by us. Thanks Amazon!

So we lose a few prospective readers at this stage too, unfortunately. Readers *we* dragged there, just to rub some vinegar into the wound.

Okay, before we get too down, let's run over this again. You know when you hear about a book from one place or another, and think it sounds interesting, look for it on Amazon, or click the link to the article, and then… hesitate? This is the Consideration Stage, when a reader is actually on your product page at the retailer of their choice and is weighing up whether to purchase. A lot of factors will feed into that decision.

If it's an author unknown to that reader, and they haven't already received a recommendation compelling enough for them to insta-buy, then the book's cover is the most important factor when they are weighing a purchase. In fact, whether you like this or not, every other factor—things like the blurb, title, sample, and price, of course—is way in the distance, though it's still important to have those in the best shape possible. We'll go into depth about how to optimize all of these, but perhaps the biggest challenge of all isn't something you might do right or wrong; it's all the other things competing for attention, even on your own product pages.

Self-publishers who have an advanced mailing list strategy know exactly what a perfect landing page looks like. There are no distractions, no clickaways. Attention is focused on one thing only: the email sign-up. It's the only escape from the page; there's nothing else for the reader to click on. The message is very focused, stressing the offer—whether that's exclusive deals and news, or a free book, or some other kind of reader magnet or bonus for signing up, or whatever. The normal navigation bar will not be present. There will be no other book covers in the sidebar, or some feed showing your latest tweets (or celebrity nip slips). Those things might normally have value on the rest of your site, but a truly optimized sign-up page only allows readers to do one thing: sign up to your list.

Amazon regularly tests different iterations and for-mats, particularly when it comes to ads and other offers it displays on our product pages, but, as I write these words, there are currently 248 different titles on the product page of the Kindle edition of *Let's Get Digital*. Between the ads, Also Boughts, Also Vieweds, Amazon promotions, and other links, there are hundreds of things that could distract a reader before they purchase.

The amount of real estate I "own" on that page gets smaller every year. Even the product description itself is now largely hidden these days, and readers must click on a prompt to see the whole thing—that space is now given over to ads for other books. We can obsess over this, or we can just deal with it. Even before ads become so widespread on our pages, there were still Also Boughts and any number of distractions. Our job remains the same: close the damn sale.

The fight to get readers to your product page can be a tricky one, but it's not the end of the struggle: you still need to seal the deal. All these distractions will become like background noise if your book is attractive enough to the readers you are driving to the page. The only difference these days is that the distractions are louder and more numerous.

Which means your presentation must be *tight*. You need an arresting blurb. Now that only the first few lines appear above the fold, you really can't bury the lede. The price should be high enough for you to make some money, of course, but low enough that readers don't hesitate. With all the flashy distractions, if they think twice you might lose them. The cover must absolutely be right for the genre—100% nailed—with no room for doubts. If you have any worries that your cover is not quite good enough or not quite right for your niche, you need to look at it again. The whole package must explicitly and exclusively target the right readers, screaming "this is the kind of book you *love*." Suboptimal presentation can lead to losing a lot of people at this stage, which is expensive, as you paid (one way or the other) to bring them here.

There's no point plunking down $400 on ads or $2,000 on a Facebook campaign if you're going to have a crappy conversion rate. There's a huge spread at this stage. Many of the factors influencing conversion rates will be outside your direct control, so it's crucial that you're getting maximum benefit from those you can affect.

In other words, your presentation must be *pristine*.

# 8: Purchase Pains

As any insecure writer will know, taking a reader's money isn't the end of your worries. That book that almost cost you your life—okay, that story that was somewhat difficult to write yet turned out somewhat amazing and more-or-less free of error—is now sitting on that reader's Kindle, unopened. Several months later. Which sounds a little ungrateful. They have your book, you have their money. Commerce happened. No one owes anything here.

This is the Purchase stage, but the Reader Journey doesn't end here. We must explore that weird alchemy by which a customer becomes a superfan, a reader who converts others into readers, and so on in a zombie-esque logarithmic orgy.

If only it were that easy.

Jane Reader has downloaded your book but is stubbornly refusing to read the damn thing. You have her $3.99—which is cool, money is handy. But you won't get any further benefit from that sale if she never reads it and never becomes a fan. Even if Jane does happen to start the book, there's a one in two chance she won't finish it—whether that's down to Jane hating the book or getting distracted by her commuter train screeching to an unexpected halt, her kids setting the cat on fire, or the never-ending klaxon of >>BREAKING NEWS<<.

While I did my best to distract you, I'm sure many fixated right away on that putative read through rate, aghast at the thought of losing as much as 50% of their readers to the most dreaded acronym of all: DNF. Let me put your mind at ease: great writers fall short of that mark *all the time*. Kobo released some very interesting figures some time ago, showing that 40% was actually a good readthrough rate and 50% was generally considered to be exceptional.

My own experience as a reader tallies with this. I *was* a lot more bloody-minded as a paperback purchaser and would invariably see a book through to the bitter end, even if I was hating every single word. I'm a lot more skittish with ebooks. If something doesn't jibe with my own personal tastes—the voice bugs me, there are major plot holes, too much head-hopping, whatever—then I'm quite likely to ditch it. No doubt this is an easier decision to make while holding a device containing hundreds of other options and a link to a store with millions more.

Reader analytics confirm all this further. Jellybooks is a company that offers readers free ARCs of new releases from publishers like Penguin Random House, Simon & Schuster, and Sourcebooks, as well as some academic publishers, and then tracks reader behavior (with their explicit consent, of course). In return, those publishers get all sorts of fascinating insights about whether readers finished a given title, how many days they took to complete it, how long each reading session was, and what devices they read on—but also at what exact point unsatisfied readers set the book aside, never to return. As the *New York Times* put it in a recent profile:

"Publishers and writers are still in the dark about what actually happens when readers pick up a book. Do most people devour it in a single sitting, or do half of readers give up after Chapter 2? Are women over 50 more likely to finish the book than young men? Which passages do they highlight, and which do they skip?"

Some of the insights that Jellybooks founder Andrew Rhomberg has shared with the industry at large have been very interesting indeed. Business books, for example, have markedly low completion rates. It seems that most readers take in a few chapters and set the book aside, confident they have already grasped the central insight (or perhaps have gleaned enough information to talk intelligently about the book in certain circles). Men are much more impatient than women, who can stick with a mediocre read for twice as long before ditching it, and women's more robust staying power is something that holds true across genres. Also, confirming that Kobo readers are no outliers when it comes to switching things up, "fewer than half of the books tested were finished by a majority of readers," the *New York Times* notes in its profile on Jellybooks.

Data from Jellybooks also confirms long-held suspicions about the differences between categories, and the speed at which those books are consumed. Romance readers can get their happy ending in just three to six days, those who prefer literary fiction will dawdle over those words for a week or three, while non-fiction tends to be completed at the comparatively sluggish pace of up to six weeks.

Whatever you write, don't assume you have won the battle just because you made the sale. The sad truth is that most readers won't finish your book.

I don't want to end on a sour note, so let me just point out that recent figures suggest that the world's Giant Panda population has increased 16.8%.

# 9: Advocacy Issues

Your Ideal Reader has seen your book, bought it, read it, and enjoyed it too. You sealed the deal, landed the plane, hit the spot, sated their hunger, slaked their thirst. Your Ideal Reader is laying back, smoking a post-coital cigarette, feeling remarkably good about what just happened. Perhaps good enough to share their happiness with the world.

But perhaps not. Hard to say for sure. What I can say is that moment is what I like to call Peak Reader Love. In other words, your reader's opinion of you is never going to be higher than it is right now. You did your job, gave them a compelling narrative, and didn't screw up the ending; now they're sad the book is finished, and they miss their book-friends.

They want more, in other words.

Which means it's the perfect time to ask them for something: mailing list sign-up, purchase of the sequel, website visit, Facebook Like, review—these are the kind of things that authors can (and should) ask for at this point. If you are ever going to convert them into an advocate for your work, that has to happen now—or that *process* must begin now.

If fewer than half the people who actually start your book aren't even going to see your end matter—because they don't get that far—then it better be in good shape. You can't afford to lose too many at this final stage; the crowd has thinned enough. Which means we need our end matter to be *slick*, so it converts as many people as possible. If we are asking readers to leave the cozy fugue state engendered by our wonderful narrative, and travel to our website and sign up to our mailing list, then the process damn well better be frictionless.

Not least because we are asking for even more than that. We're probably looking for the purchase of another book, as well as a sign-up, and perhaps a Facebook Like or Twitter follow as well. Even the most stripped back end-matter is going to be asking for two or three favors from a reader, so we want to make it straightforward, but enticing.

Ultimately, the aim is to have superfans advocating for us, selling books on our behalf, all while we spend our time working on the next. You can engineer any number of sales with smart marketing, but it's even better to have a reader army doing the evangelizing for you, as nothing is more compelling than a fellow reader recommending a book.

# PART III
# OPTIMIZING THE READER JOURNEY

Now we'll get our hands dirty. We understand the problem, and have mapped out the Reader Journey, highlighting potential pitfalls at each stage: discoverability myths, visibility chokepoints, consideration distraction, purchase pains, and advocacy issues. Now we are ready to tackle the escalating challenge of conversion. Which sounds kind of like an indie author boss fight…

# 10: The Escalating Challenge of Conversion

Conversion is hard. I've mentioned a couple of times that we focus too much on the Discovery stage, and the size of that error will become apparent here as we look at the five stages again. When we successfully subject our Ideal Reader to our marketing contraptions and word-spells, they undergo a metamorphosis, shedding their stranger-caterpillar skins to become majestic superfan-butterflies. In these initial chapters I've described each stage of Discovery, Visibility, Consideration, Purchase, and Advocacy, and mentioned some of the problems that each stage can pose. My contention here is a little more daring, perhaps: each stage represents an escalating challenge of conversion.

As I mentioned earlier, it's something like querying an agent and thinking that one "yes" is all you need. Because even if our imaginary agent likes your book and signs you on the spot, you have only passed the *first* hurdle. Your book still needs to be "sold" several more times. That hard-to-get agent must then sell your book to an acquiring editor. The editor must win hearts and minds internally to convince marketing to back it. The sales force must woo the buyers for book chains. And then the floor staff of the bookseller must try to actually flog it to flesh-and-blood readers.

To put it another way, there are lots of points where one can fall short—and most books obligingly do! Similarly, each stage of The Reader Journey also represents a potential failure point. You have to be a fully paid-up member of the Grand Fraternity of Cynics to describe a sales opportunity as a potential failure point, but I digress. Sometimes it's hard to discern the reasons someone progressed from interest to click, but then opted not to purchase. But other times it's not, and you should move swiftly and ruthlessly to rectify any issues you can identify.

With that in mind, I want to posit something. As you might well be able to recite in your sleep at this point, there are five main stages in The Reader Journey—Discovery, Visibility, Consideration, Purchase, and Advocacy—and I think the hazards increase at each stage. I call this the escalating challenge of conversion, which underlines the danger of focusing exclusively on the Discovery stage… or thinking your job ends at the Purchase stage, two common traps for authors.

Perhaps because it's the first problem we encounter—one which seems so daunting when starting from zero—but we tend to obsess with the Discovery stage at the expense of almost everything else. When we want to address lackluster sales, we always reach for Discovery solutions, forgetting about other possible problems. This is dangerous. We may have a Visibility problem or a Purchase problem but are treating it as a Discovery problem and pouring more and more expensive traffic into a broken system.

You may disagree, but I contend that each stage represents a trickier challenge—and that's undeniably true if you continue to underestimate post-Discovery issues. If the failure point is actually located further down the line, throwing traffic (i.e. money) at it will just result in ever-decreasing ROI—as well as one big wasted opportunity.

Yikes. We moved pretty quickly there from clap-happy to "Goodbye, cruel world!"

Don't be too disheartened. It's important to map out the problem comprehensively before attacking it, and I'm sure your mind is already circling some solutions. But let's tackle all this in a systematic way so we can learn to close the sale at each stage *like a boss*.

If any further motivation were needed to put yourself in your Ideal Readers' shoes and look at each stage of the Reader Journey from their perspective, here are some fairly typical conversion rates. Before you freak out, remember: conversion is *hard*.

Readers on your list are probably your most engaged—your core audience, or a good chunk of them. The open rate on your list could be anything from 30% to 60% or more, depending on a whole bunch of variables, including how you have treated those readers historically (something we'll talk about in detail later). The click rate could be anything from 1% to 20% or more, depending on a similar bunch of variables. The percentage I'm specifically interested in right here is the conversion rate of those happy, engaged, *core readers* who have already opened and clicked your email and have arrived on the Amazon product page of your brand-new release. 60% is fairly typical. That's right, you'll lose 40% at this stage of even your most loyal, engaged, *motivated* readers.

If you manage to bag a BookBub Featured Deal, you are tapping into one of the most responsive, happy, engaged audiences of book buyers out there. I've seen conversion rates come in at around 50% for these highly curated deals—again strictly talking about those readers who actually make it to the Amazon product page, not speaking to their open and click rates beforehand, or anything else that isn't immediately relevant here. The BookBub Ads at the bottom of the email can get a conversion rate of around 25% (out of the small percentage who do click). Facebook Ads might get 20% converting, and Amazon Ads a touch less, in my experience—maybe 15%.

Obviously, these are aggregate estimates and not written in stone at all—there will be huge variables in each individual case. These rough numbers are purely for illustrative purposes, to show you that, out of the tiny fraction of people you target who do actually progress to your Amazon page, most won't purchase. And that pattern continues *inside the book*. A good readthrough rate is around 40%. Most people won't even finish your book! Most won't even see that end-matter you've fretted over. Which means you really must close the emotional sale with those who do.

It can be quite daunting when you chain all these potential failure points together and consider typical conversion rates. But it's also a giant opportunity; optimizing each stage can have a huge cumulative effect.

So let's do that.

# 11: Getting Discovered

I've said that a Discovery problem is easy to solve, and it's also easy to screw up. Anyone can buy traffic and point it towards a book. But we're not Coke or Apple. We're not selling products with such broad appeal. Our business is ridiculously balkanized—the biggest seller of the year might be read by less than 1% of the book buying public—which is why marketers coming in from the outside often struggle to get a handle on it. We don't want a traffic hose; we must be more discriminate—to cultivate super-qualified leads, in marketing parlance. Readers' tastes are ridiculously niche, but that's a good thing, as this fractured market means that many more of us can individually grab a piece of it.

This should guide us when seeking out our Ideal Readers, but this is where writers are their own worst enemies. You might know your book predominantly appeals to middle-aged men, but can't help experimenting with running some ads to a slightly younger crowd, thinking there might be a little crossover.

You must be strict with yourself, with your ad spend

and targeting. Because the Discovery problem is so easy to solve (anyone can buy an ad), that means it's also easy to solve incorrectly. The danger here is considerable. If you start funneling the wrong readers through, you might look at tepid sales and misdiagnose the problem and change things that are working for you! Disaster.

Better to get it right from the start, which means being ruthless about exclusively targeting the right readers. But what does that mean, really? It means not rolling anyone into your audience who might be ambivalent about your work. You need to exclusively focus on *your* people. Your Ideal Readers.

Luckily, today's ad platforms give us a variety of options for doing just that. Certain deal sites like Ereader News Today allow readers to select which genres they are exclusively interested in and enable authors to only advertise to those eyeballs. Some genre-specific sites like BookBarbarian, Book Adrenaline, and Red Feather Romance exclusively focus on certain niches. (By the way, if you want my personal recommendations when it comes to deal sites like this, including a list of genre specialists, check out the Resources page for this book at *DavidGaughran.com/SuperfansResources*.)

Platforms like Facebook, BookBub, and Amazon Ads allow you to be even more precise, drilling right down to target fans of a certain author or series. Often the clicks are more expensive here, but in return you get two things that are hard to get elsewhere: that granular targeting plus scale.

It would require a dedicated book to give you a step-by-step guide to advertising on Facebook, but let me explain a little of how I use the platform to ensure I'm only targeting the right readers, and how knowledge of my Ideal Reader informs my use of the platform. This will be most useful for those already with some Facebook experience. For everyone else, I regularly cover the subject in my weekly newsletters—which you can sign up to at *DavidGaughran.com*.

Those who have been advertising on Facebook for a while will know that it used to be quite straightforward to target an author in your niche on Facebook, but that option is becoming more and more difficult. I think Facebook was getting heat from early adopter brands that had done all the early running on the platform, and then the market leader could just swoop in and blow you away. For example, if you were Pepsi and you spotted an opportunity on Facebook first, and spent a fair bit of cash and manpower figuring out the platform and identifying all your target market, you might be pretty sore if Coke came along a couple of years later and just targeted your hard-earned Likes.

Facebook has been nudging us towards other forms

of targeting instead, which aren't quite as granular. Still useful, of course, but you can't always drill down to the specific reader niche you might want in the way you can do elsewhere. There are lots of other powerful things you can do on Facebook, of course, which make up for that limitation. I'm getting a lot of joy with things like video-led awareness campaigns at the moment, and that's enabling me to develop my own custom audiences that I can retarget with successive campaigns.

I can understand why my Ideal Reader is more responsive to these campaigns. She doesn't really like when her first interaction with someone finishes with some kind of ask. I call this serving hard ads to cold people—when their first experience of you is asking for their money. I often prefer to warm up this cold audience with some content first, either video or other content they might enjoy. The advantage with video is that you have amazing re-targeting options—such as segmenting those who have watched 45 seconds of a minute-long video, and only hitting them with an ask. I know these are the most engaged viewers, and the most likely to purchase something. The much-improved CTRs and conversion rates most certainly back this up.

BookBub has its own limitations of course—all platforms do—but it allows you to explicitly target a specific author's audience in a very straightforward way.

Terminology can be a little confusing, so I'll stick with BookBub's nomenclature. BookBub Featured Deals are the heavily curated spots in the deals email sent out to millions of readers every day, and which you must apply for (and few are accepted). BookBub Ads is the open-to-all advertising platform.

BookBub Ads allow you to target the followers of any author in their (very comprehensive) system, which means you can explicitly target your Ideal Readers. I gave the example earlier of how drilling down to Patrick O'Brian's followers on BookBub, rather than just hitting their Historical Fiction list, turned a losing ad into a winner: the cost per click went from $2 to around 25¢. I was able to make this change by considering my Ideal Reader's tastes within the broad church that is Historical Fiction.

By the way, if you want to get deeper into BookBub Ads specifically, I have a dedicated book on the topic called *BookBub Ads Expert*. I have a free course covering the basics too, and you can get information on both of those at the Resources page on my website for this book at *DavidGaughran.com/SuperfansResources*.

With Amazon Ads, you can explicitly target certain authors, and even book and series titles. Again, success with Amazon Ads is helped by imagining your Ideal Reader actually looking for a book on Amazon. She might be a huge Nora Roberts fan, but might not know the exact name of her last release, or whether she released something else in the interim she might have missed. She might search for something like "Nora Roberts new release" or "Nora Roberts 2020."

The key point in covering all these platforms is this: we have incredibly sophisticated targeting options at our fingertips, which we should use to drill down to our Ideal Readers as much as we can. But we must also remember what things look like on the other side of the curtain and imagine how readers use these platforms on the customer side.

Aside from reader sites and ads, there are a whole swath of ways to get discovered. It's beyond the scope of this book to go through them all exhaustively, but the following strategies and tactics usually prove fruitful.

Price promotions are simple but powerful, especially when paired with advertising. They can be as simple as making a book free or 99¢ and taking out an ad on a reader site, or as complex as running a variety of discounts across a whole series and hitting different pockets of readers on Facebook, BookBub, and Amazon simultaneously.

Permafree is a pretty evergreen strategy too. It can be as basic as just making the first book in your series free to encourage new readers to try it, hoping you'll make the money back with increased sales on Book 2. And it can be more advanced too, like dangling a free book to encourage mailing list sign-ups, one which is delivered as part of an optimized automation sequence that will (gently) weed out the freeloaders while delighting your Ideal Reader, and subsequently converting them into the kind of superfan who opens each email—and buys each new release—the moment it hits her inbox. More on that later.

Cross-promotion is very powerful too, and can be as straightforward as an author in the same niche recommending your books to their audience. This too can reach layers of sophistication, like any tactic, and authors can arrange newsletter swaps, or do themed box sets together, and advertise repeatedly to each other's audience to create a web of Also Boughts that can act like chain lightning—promotion rippling through each title when any book gets a sales spike.

At all times, though, you want to be aiming at readers who are squarely in your target audience. If you are running out of road with one tactic, be careful about widening your scope; it's often better to switch tactics instead, because there are endless ways to get discovered… and even more ways to do it incorrectly.

# 12: Increasing Visibility

There are so many simple things you can do to increase visibility that cost you nothing more than a few clicks, and collectively they can make a huge difference in your footprint on Amazon, especially during a sales spike. This is the unsexy grunt work that many ignore at the expense of pursuing flasher initiatives. What these people foolishly forget is that optimizing for visibility is a one-off job that will add a considerable sales halo to every single promotion you run in the future.

Maximizing your visibility on Amazon means both understanding how the Kindle Store works and optimizing your metadata based on that knowledge. Which sounds incredibly boring, but I promise it's not! I have a dedicated book called *Amazon Decoded* which goes into great detail on this topic, which will be especially useful for experienced self-publishers. But you can also get the basics from reading a handful of (free) articles on my website—the links are all on the Resources page for this book at *DavidGaughran.com/SuperfansResources*.

*Amazon Decoded* is the only book out there, to my

knowledge, that breaks down how the Kindle Store works and how you can arrange your promotions to take advantage of algorithms that power the recommendation engine, so you will get multiple benefits from reading it. Right now, though, I want you to particularly focus on the importance of keywords and categories, and how smart choices can ensure that you appear on many more of those millions of visibility spots around the Amazon site, introducing you to even more new readers every time you run a promotion. Smart keyword choices will dramatically expand your categories, which will in turn multiply your footprint in the world's biggest bookstore, particularly in the places readers scour looking for fresh books to read.

For example, let's imagine I have written a high fantasy about a pair of star-crossed lovers, a wise-cracking Goblin thief and Elvish princess who staves away boredom by moonlighting as… a thief catcher. Hilarity ensues! Now, I have a few options when it comes to categorizing it on Amazon. While there is an open-door sex scene that's pretty damn hot, Erotica is probably not the right category here. Neither is it Romance, even though she buys him breakfast and even calls him after. The natural home for this book is Fantasy, quite obviously, but selecting that top-level category is missing a trick. Amazon has twenty-three subcategories on offer where I can really drill down and be visible to my Ideal Reader, everything ranging from Alternative History and Arthurian Fantasy to Urban Fantasy and Superhero stories.

Those options are also a handy reminder of how diverse every genre is—yet another reason to always be as granular as possible in our targeting.

I now recommend the following approach to get into your target sub-categories. First, select the sub-categories which are the best fit for your work in the publishing interface of KDP (either when first publishing your book, or afterwards). This menu is much more limited than the Kindle Store itself. For example, here I can choose Epic Fantasy explicitly, which is great, as that's a good fit for my book. But Sword & Sorcery isn't selectable, and I'd like to be in that one; it's a little less competitive and might help me get some visibility while sales are slower.

The best practices around categories changed in 2020, and Amazon is, finally, explicit about the number of sub-categories you can have for each book: ten. The process for adding those additional categories is a little involved, and changes quite regularly too, so I have copied it out for you on the Resources page for this book at *DavidGaughran.com/SuperfansResources* instead—so I can keep it accurate and up to date for you.

Going to the same effort at the other stores won't lead to anything like the same benefits, but every little bit helps—especially outside Amazon—so make sure you are making similarly astute keyword and category choices, and maximizing those opportunities wherever you can (for example, Kobo permits three category choices and Google Play allows five; never let an opportunity for visibility go to waste, but always keep it relevant too).

# 13: Browsers to Buyers—How To Make A Product Page Convert

I was working for Google when it was just a little start-up—in Europe at least—crammed into the old Sky News office on Fitzwilliam Square in Dublin. The boss was an American guy brought over from California to get things up and running in Ireland, and he told one story that stuck with me.

When Google Search was still in beta, back in 1998, it began getting a series of cryptic emails from an unknown person. They were quite mysterious and indecipherable, containing only a single number, and they would arrive at irregular intervals. Google was full of all kinds of nerds, many with an interest in things like cryptography, but no one could crack the code, and the mystery sender wasn't talking. The only discernible pattern was that this number was increasing. Quite some time passed before one engineer realized the answer was very simple indeed: it corresponded to the exact number of words on the Google.com homepage.

Think of that homepage: a white rectangle, simple

and elegant like an Apple store, almost Zen-like—just a basic search box and a couple of buttons. Many have copied its design since, but in 1998 all the established players in the search business looked very different. Yahoo's search box, for example, was surrounded by all sorts of extraneous crap: Oracle's share price, the weather in Tokyo, Pamela Anderson's wedding photos. All of which might have been of little interest to you, and a distraction from what you really wanted to do—which was find the nearest place serving fish tacos *right now*.

Google was pure, minimalist, exact, putting order on the chaos of the web. At least, it gave off that impression very successfully indeed.

What relevance does this have to you? Take a look at your Amazon product page today. Contrast that with how it looked back in 2012, for example. It's a *lot* busier; there are hundreds of different ways for readers to click away from your product page that don't involve hitting that Buy button.

Why would Amazon do this? Because its goals are different than yours. You want that immediate sale. Amazon is happy to sell anything; money is money. Or to put it another way, Amazon wants to ensure readers buy the book they want the most, so will dangle *lots* of shiny alternatives in the background while you are trying to close your sale. I guess we shouldn't grouse too much, as it cuts both ways! The effect, however, is something we definitely do need to manage.

You all know what a fully optimized sign-up page looks like. It has no clickaways. There's only one thing a user can do to escape this page, and that's give up their email. Well, I guess they could hurl their laptop into the nearest canal, but you get my point. An Amazon product page is the polar opposite of this. There are so many distractions that you can't afford to be anything other than super slick in how you present your work, eliminating any possible failure points, anything that might make a reader hesitate before clicking that glorious Buy button.

I think sometimes authors have an attitude of "they'll either buy it or they won't," which is a gross simplification. Successive tests of different covers and blurbs and samples and price points show that there is a huge range at this stage. Buy rates can be anything from 0% to 50% or more depending on the quality of the traffic, and the appeal of those conversion factors: author name, reviews, blurbs, price, award mentions, bestseller status, cover, and sample.

We can be incredibly lazy with some of these elements. Let's take blurbs, for example. We spend so much time slaving over our book, or reworking our intro, and so little on what could be the real intro to the book for new-to-you readers: the paragraph or three of text on your Amazon product page. Or we settle for the first half-assed formulation we come up with. Really though, unless you are a naturally skilled or very experienced blurb writer, it will take several drafts to get something that is truly enticing to your Ideal Reader.

Each one of these conversion elements should get the same level of focus from you, as every single one is an opportunity to hook your reader. Don't believe me? Let's take a less obvious example: the title. *Love in the Time of Cholera* may not excite you personally, but it gives a frisson of excitement to the target market of Gabriel Garcia Marquez. I'm not the Ideal Reader for *Pride & Prejudice & Zombies*, but I don't need to be to see how cleverly the title will appeal.

Aside from visceral reader appeal, titles can often do some more prosaic heavy lifting for you. The subtitle of my book *Let's Get Digital* is quite a mouthful: *How To Self-Publish, And Why You Should*. The first part is a naked attempt to appear higher in Amazon Search for important terms my Ideal Reader will be searching for— one that works very nicely too—but it's combined with something else so it can also act as a conversion element for browsers of my product page. The book is aimed at people who don't just want to know *how* to do something, but to get the logic behind it also, i.e. the *why*. Never miss a trick, is what I'm saying, and that goes for all your conversion elements.

It's a bit more work, yes. But, like optimizing your keywords and categories, you only have to do it once, and you'll benefit from it as long as your book is on sale.

# 14: DNF to OMG

We all love different things, which is what makes the world interesting. We all hate different things too, which is what creates so many passionate discussions. Hooray for that! It makes analyzing quality difficult, though, because if we can't agree on what's "good," then there's little chance of teasing out commonalities. This drives some people crazy—literally, in the case of the protagonist in *Zen and the Art of Motorcycle Maintenance*—but I'm okay with this. As an unrepentant hack who likes to eat several times a day, I'm more concerned with what's entertaining: stories that keep readers glued to the page, characters they fall in love with. And especially books they rave about.

I mentioned earlier how big the challenge is at this stage. We fret over discovery and sweat over purchase numbers, and spend little time wondering how many readers actually finish the books we have so carefully crafted. And as I explained earlier, that number is much lower than we often assume. When I'm giving workshops to authors, I often ask them what they think a good completion rate might be on a book—and they're usually shocked to hear that most readers will set their story aside without completing it.

Given the investment we make—financially and emotionally—getting our books into the hands of readers, we should probably be paying more attention to whether they actually consume the product we're selling them. Admittedly, this lack of focus isn't all on us; retailers are generally reluctant to share data with us, and Kobo is unique in divulging even the most aggregate, anonymous completion stats at various author conferences. While companies like Jellybooks go further—I spoke about the insights they have gleaned from reader analytics in Chapter 8—this kind of data isn't available to us. Not yet, at least.

And, as interesting as it may be, there's a danger of getting lost in the data here. The most relevant concern is this: how can we write better books? How can we ensure that more readers enjoy our work enough to passionately recommend it to others? Presumably getting more of them to finish the damn thing would help significantly in that regard.

Dan Brown is the author I love to hate, as many of you might know. I don't actually "hate" him—he may well be pleasant company—it's just that his prose style doesn't appeal to me whatsoever. (I'm sure his sleep will be untroubled tonight.) This is my *subjective* opinion of his work. Clearly, he's been a huge commercial success, and his fans continue to gobble up every single word he publishes, no matter what crazy price his publisher charges for a new hardback. Dan Brown's *success* is an objective fact.

This contradiction between my (unimportant) subjective opinion and his (rather more relevant) objective success led me to read a Dan Brown book. While I didn't enjoy it, *per se*, I did get through it at a blinding pace. What sorcery is this? I'm not entirely sure which Dan Brown book it was—maybe *Deception Point*; that nugget of information is lost to the sands of time. I do remember that I couldn't put it down, even though I might have wanted to!

Pacing seems to be the secret ingredient in many bestsellers that people passionately claim are poorly written; everyone has their own book or author they love to hate. These books can be vastly different in terms of prose style, but all tend to be described as "page-turners"—although that term will be used as compliment or insult, depending.

It's not so much about the specific genre; the gripping nature of a story you can't put down is something that transcends categories. It seems to be more about the *shape* of the story, the emotional beats, the pacing, the inherent and incessant forward motion. All pretty intangible, but as writers yourselves I'm sure you know what I mean.

Readers often describe it as the story getting its hooks in you and not letting go. And it's little to do with how purple (or spare) the sentences are. You may hate the writing but be unable to help seeing how the story turns out! Giant bestsellers invariably have this in common—the overarching compulsion to finish, not necessarily the part about hating the writing style. Many bestsellers are very well written indeed (in my subjective opinion).

What varies quite significantly in genre terms are the respective tropes. Romance fans demand a HEA (but may settle for a HFN). Historical fiction readers insist on at least some properly researched level of authenticity in the setting. Mysteries must have a crime to be solved that readers can puzzle over. And so on. This isn't writers being unimaginative, it's part of what is often referred to as writing to market. Of course, you can write a romance where the couple don't hook up or a mystery about where someone left their car keys, but you might have trouble selling that to readers. This doesn't mean you can't be creative, of course; a lot of fun can be had playing with conventions and subverting them too.

I'm not going to tell you what to write, or how to write. But I will suggest that you respect the conventions of the genre you are working in. And ensure that readers are captivated from the first line to the last. If you want to sell, that is.

As much as we may wish to educate readers about what really caused World War I, or why it can be hard to trust again after an abusive relationship, or how our political system will look once we're all spending eighteen hours a day in virtual reality, the Jellybooks data is abundantly clear on one key point: the books with the highest completion rates—which are read the fastest and recommended the most passionately—are not those that teach them something, necessarily, or the ones they feel some obligation or social pressure to read, or even the books that make them look smart because they won some big literary award.

The books readers finish are the ones they find most entertaining.

# 15: Handing Out Megaphones

Turning readers from people who enjoyed your work into advocates who recommend it to others requires two things. One is incredibly simple; you can implement it today—hooray! The other is incredibly difficult and will be an ongoing job for as long as you are writing and releasing. But hold off on that sad trombone; you will also benefit from it over your entire career.

Let's start with the first.

Your end matter is so important—it's the first exchange with your Ideal Reader after they finish. And if your end matter isn't in good shape, it might also be the *last* exchange you have with that reader. This is super basic, but important enough to bear repeating—and always worth reviewing to make sure you are maximizing the possibilities.

A reader wants one thing when they finish a great book: more. If you have more to give them, make sure a link to that is the first thing they see—just keep in mind that they will probably define that more narrowly than you would like. In practical terms this means a link to

Book 2 should be the first thing your readers see after The End. If Book 2 isn't out yet, then it should be a link to your mailing list—rather than, for example, a link to that standalone that's *kind of* in the same niche.

You can mention other books afterwards, and all the other things you might like to include in your end matter, such as a review request, a mailing list sign-up if you haven't asked for that already, a link to your site or Facebook Page or Twitter profile, or whatever else might be important to you and your readership. In general, I think you should be present where your readers like to hang out and *at the very least* have a profile on the social networks they favor so that they can communicate with you where *they* are most comfortable.

This doesn't mean you have to be pouring time into building up a presence on Pinterest and LinkedIn and Google+ and every single network out there. But if your readers are big on Twitter, then I think you should, at the very least, have a presence there. I don't think Twitter is a great tool for building audience in most cases. Rather, you can use this in a reactive/passive way. It's also important for another reason: you are giving readers easy tools to share your work. If a reader is following you on Twitter or Facebook and sees your announcement of a 99¢ sale or new release, they are much more likely to share it when all they have to do is click a button.

Optimized end matter is pretty much a one-off job. You might need to review it every so often, but it's a small amount of effort for a continuous pay-off.

Deepening connections with those readers over time, however, is another matter.

Building a long-term relationship with your readership is done in two ways. Well, three ways, if you count continuing to release books they love—the most important of all, of course. That aside, social media and email will be your two primary methods of communication with readers. And I want you to think of these readers—those who follow you on Facebook or who have signed up to your mailing list—as your core readers.

Over time, we can fall into a trap of mistreating our core readers. It happens slowly, without us even noticing, and without any malice whatsoever. A typical example: a writer can engage in various promotions to find new readers, a box set here, a free run there. Often, they don't share these deals with their established readership, fearing reader reaction, or worried about cannibalizing lucrative full-price sales. Readers can get annoyed when they pay full price for a book and then see it reduced to 99¢ the following week. Sometimes that's a little unfair—all businesses engage in promotions—but they can have a point. There are a few authors who can be a little too aggressive and run steep discounts just a few weeks after a launch. Core readers can, rightly, feel a little cheated.

You can avoid this by always making sure you are providing value to your core readership. Don't be afraid to tell them about deals—it's better hearing it from you than from Amazon or BookBub. Social media is a great way of communicating with readers, and I recommend that you are always present where you readers hang out, but I think the ultimate aim should always be to get as many of your core readers onto your list as possible.

Facebook and other forms of social media can be excellent ways of finding new readers, communicating with existing ones, and deepening those relationships overall. However, email should be the primary way you choose to communicate with your core readership, because email has the following advantages:

1. **Ownership.** Facebook lets you write on your Page's timeline, but most of your audience won't see the post unless you pay, and the price is rising all the time. Twitter doesn't even let you pay to reach all your followers. You can advertise there, but only in a broader sense. Good luck finding your dweeby follower-needles in the giant haystacks of Twitter!

2. **Attention.** When you are reading an email, there's way less distraction than when reading a

post on social media. You are much more likely to get readers to respond to an ask in an email than a social media post, which is crucial for something like a new release. A good CTR on a Facebook ad might be 2%-4%. A good click rate on email is more like 20%. The teeny buttons on your calculator watch may remain untroubled here because the difference is clear.

3. **Intimacy.** A public post is inherently and explicitly for a broad audience. While an email might theoretically be sent to thousands of people, it feels to the reader much more like organic two-way communication, and allows you to deepen the connection with that person (especially if you write it that way—take note). Of course, readers can also respond to your email and then you will have an actual two-way communication, which will further deepen that connection in much more tangible way.

4. **Data.** I know who opens my emails, and who clicks. Facebook gives very little away, and only aggregate, anonymized info, or little morsels like who has Liked something. I have no idea who viewed my post and didn't click, and certainly have no way to segment that slice of the population to try a different approach.

5. **Flexibility.** If someone doesn't open five emails in a row, I can move them onto a different list, and try to re-engage them while also giving them a very clear opportunity to unsubscribe—a great way to arrest falling open rates. No social network will allow you to do this, which becomes a problem over time because some level of natural wastage is inevitable no matter how great your content is. Those now-uninterested Likes keep accumulating like mercury in your body, adding to the overall cost of reaching your still-interested Likes, dampening your overall engagement levels, and convincing Facebook's algorithms that your content isn't that interesting—which further pushes up your costs and reduces your organic reach.

6. **Portability.** If Twitter goes to the wall, so do my 25,000 followers and all the connections I've assiduously developed. Now let's say Mailchimp does the same, or merges with another company, or changes its policies, or jacks up its prices, or the service otherwise deteriorates. I'm not trapped. I have options. Particularly this one: I can take my list, ride off into the sunset, and then dramatically collapse into the digital embrace of another.

Social media has inherent advantages too; there's little chance of an email going viral. But in terms of deepening connections with your readers and turning them into superfans, there is no contest. While Facebook can aid and abet that process, I think your ultimate goal should always be to shepherd as many people as possible onto your list.

Savvy authors are always looking for the next way to reach readers—free runs, price promotions, BookBub Deals, Facebook Ads, Amazon Ads, Kindle Unlimited— but there is a danger of becoming too reliant on one marketing tactic… and then seeing sales collapse when it's no longer viable. The best way to futureproof your career is to focus on your mailing list, and on getting as many of your core readers on there as possible. I once wrote a post called *The Author With The Biggest Mailing List Wins*, but you aren't supposed to take the title literally. It's much better to have a smaller, engaged list than a large and unresponsive one. In other words, what happens to those core readers *after* they sign up to your list is most important of all.

I used to be terrible at email—I did all the don'ts. So many horrendous mistakes! First, I had one mailing list for all my output, even though there's little crossover between historical fiction and writerly advice. Which meant one tranche of my list was getting assailed with amped-up launch emails about marketing whizzbangery when all they really wanted was another novel set in a far-flung locale. And I'm sure the writers were wondering why I kept banging on about blood-based racism in colonial Peru. That was some oily water.

Second, while I thought I was being considerate by not bothering people between launches, this is what was really happening: I was only emailing them when I wanted something. That "thing" might have been a new book they were excited about (at least half the time, see above), but an unbroken string of asks has a cumulative effect; you can go from excited booty call recipient to feeling used pretty quickly. One hears.

Third, I'm slow. Not just generally, but specifically as a writer too—those historical novels in particular. Readers forgot who I was between books. I almost forgot myself! I wasn't keeping them engaged, they weren't remaining interested, readers had moved on… probably to other authors who were producing faster, or at the very least were keeping in touch now and then.

Fourth, I'm not *that* slow. I guess I knew deep down that I wasn't keeping people engaged and wasn't providing value in each email, and that I was just chaining together a string of needy asks like whatever the opposite of a charm bracelet is. My subconscious knew the truth. This manifested itself in apologetic, eyes-down emails—which is no way to communicate, let alone launch a book.

And the people responded! My email list stopped growing. Unsubscribes rose. But the biggest effect was a much more insidious one: the slow creeping rot that is declining open and click rates.

Unlike gangrene, however, this can be reversed. When I adopted a new approach at the beginning of 2018, I was able to turn all that around. My email list grew by 600%—a very clear signal that I had chosen the correct path.

You can find a link to lots and lots more resources on raising your email game and capturing reader interest, on the Resources page for this book at *DavidGaughran. com/SuperfansResources.* In very general terms, though, what I did differently was to treat my subscribers like people, instead of names on a list. I tried to give first, instead of only asking. I kept in touch regularly, instead of only knocking on their door when I needed something. I now have the means to develop genuine and meaningful relationships with my readers; it has been transformative.

## Advocacy Through Branding

Email isn't the only way to nurture those relationships. Indeed, this process can often start much earlier than at the point of email capture and doesn't need to involve an email sign-up at all. Just look at global phenomena like Harry Potter or *Twilight*—books that have created legions of passionate fans, who won't just buy all the books and rave about them to anyone who listen, but get the t-shirt too. How can you tap into some of *those* feelings? Is it even possible to engineer or encourage that kind of passion in your readership? Well, maybe.

I can see the immediate objections from some authors and, yes, there's always going to be a genre angle to this. It's far more likely that readers of paranormal romance are going to run around proclaiming their loyalty to Team Edward versus Team Other Guy, or that fans of Harry Potter will proudly declare which House they are in, than that they will have a poster of Gregor Samsa from *Metamorphosis* on their wall or empathize with the talking cat from Murakami's *Kafka on the Shore*. So it goes.

But that doesn't mean that writers of all stripes can't learn something from studying fandom, and what stimulates those feelings in readers. One of the most powerful sensations a reader can experience is that feeling of losing close friends when they hit The End—it's so visceral that it can move some to tears. Not me, obviously—I have the empathic qualities of your average aircon unit. But I spoke to fully operational human being Kit Rocha, who has a whole legion of passionate superfans, about attracting and engaging them in fascinating ways.

The first thing you notice when you look at Kit Rocha's books is the branding is *tight*. If pacing is the secret sauce inside most bestsellers, branding is the equivalent outside of the book. It's the same with many bestsellers; they seem to have a certain intangible quality, which is usually that all elements of the presentation are in harmony and pulling in one direction. This is no accident. As Kit Rocha put it to me: "Branding is an extension of worldbuilding. My covers and my graphics and all of it combine to present an image that enhances what I want to say about my series."

If you look at Kit Rocha's Facebook Page, you won't just see a thriving, passionate reader community, but that super-tight branding that trickles all the way down to the promotional graphics she uses to kickstart group discussions. The themes and tropes in her stories are also reinforced through judicious selection of taglines. This doesn't just double down on the message she would like to impart to readers, it also signals to potential fans that this is the kind of book they would like. It conveys a sense of belonging, which is what fandom is all about, at its heart—that you are hanging with *your people*.

I asked Kit whether email or Facebook (or Twitter,

which she uses religiously) was more important to her for communicating with her readers, and she said something very interesting indeed: "I consider everything I do worldbuilding. The specific mode of communication isn't as important as having a cohesive brand—little details can mean a lot in maintaining an atmosphere." Ultimately, though, for Kit it starts with the story itself. "There are types of stories that really work well with this, ones where readers want to belong to your world."

All of this is very genuine, and not contrived in any way. Kit Rocha has such a clear picture of her Ideal Reader that she instinctively knows her readers' likes and dislikes, because she is one of those people too. And because her fans feel a part of what she is doing, they want her books to succeed. They want to expand their tribe to find others who are lost, wandering the woods, looking for their people. She even empowers her readers by creating promotional assets that she doles out during launch week, making sure her army of advocates are on brand too—something we can all learn from.

# PART IV
# THE FAILURE MATRIX

You are my Ideal Reader, which means that I know you are a person of impeccable taste, glamorous, cosmopolitan, intelligent… and incredibly busy. The Failure Matrix was designed with you in mind, to help you identify where the failure points are in your back catalog, so you can quickly locate blockages in your Reader Journey. But to do that, you're going to need to learn more about failures at each stage and how to identify one kind from another. It's time to delve into failure in all its glorious forms!

# 16: Locating Failure Points

I'm going to take a wild stab in the dark here and guess that you don't have enough hours in the day. We can be required to wear many hats: writer, storyteller, publisher, CEO, marketer, social media expert, growth hacker, blogger, and email engagement ninja. Underneath all that, an artist's heart is still beating, one hopes. This can be time-consuming, and that's before you get into whatever commitments you have outside of work. You may have dependents who need care of one kind or another, illnesses or physical conditions that need to be managed, possibly a second job to juggle, and then I'm sure you also need some kind of cultural nourishment to refill the well periodically—whether that's going to a museum or watching *Firefly*.

It's tough enough to keep on top of your writing and organize promotions for your frontlist. If you have some older backlist that isn't selling and can't seem to be resuscitated, it's tempting to hang up the "Nil by Mouth" sign and focus on the rest of your catalog. For sure, releasing new work is the most powerful jolt to sales you can muster, whether your name is Stephen King or Jane Nobody, but maybe that backlist isn't *quite* dead yet.

Perhaps you threw some promotion at those books and the ROI wasn't quite there. Maybe you sold a few of your spin-off series opener but the sell-through to Book 2 wasn't there. It's easy to walk away at this point and tell yourself you're doing the right thing, but perhaps there is more juice to be squeezed here, because it's quite likely you assumed it was a Discovery problem but applying traffic didn't help. Maybe you considered changing the covers but weren't sure if you would recover the investment—which is a fair consideration.

What you really need is some kind of diagnostic tool that you can use to survey your backlist and identify what kind of problem you have, because if you knew that, you would know how to fix it. The problem here isn't so much that these issues are completely unsolvable. It's that you might be looking at a backlist of twenty or thirty distinct titles, and if you were to examine every aspect of each book and try to analyze why each individual one wasn't selling, you could go down that rabbit hole for quite some time indeed.

Unfortunately, no such diagnostic tool exists. But I'm confident that once you know the difference between a problem at the Discovery stage versus one at the

Consideration stage, you will develop a keen instinct for knowing where the issues lie, which means you can begin to optimize your backlist in a fraction of the time.

I'll give a real-world example so we don't get too conceptual here. Let's say I have a BookBub ad for the first book in my hypothetical action/adventure series *The Atlantis Paradox*. If sales are way less than expected, I might have a Consideration Fail. If sales are solid, but there is no sell-through to Book 2, it could be a Purchase Fail. Or if sales are great but there's no halo after the promotion and the book just tanks and never recovers, that could be a Visibility Fail.

Sometimes it's not so clear cut, but you can usually at least narrow it down to one or two types of problems, which radically reduces the things you need to try to get sales moving again—saving you time, money, and mental energy.

How can you develop this spidey sense? It's time to enter the Failure Matrix.

# 17: Discovery Fail

One of the problems with Discovery issues is that they are over-diagnosed. Like a doctor telling you—no matter what's wrong with you—that you could really do with losing a little weight, or getting more exercise, or eating more fruit, it's easy to reach for Discovery solutions. We could always eat more bloody fruit, and even Lee Child could probably sell a few extra Jack Reacher books if he just ran some Amazon Ads. As I've repeated many times in this book—hopefully enough for it to stick—often the *primary* problem lies elsewhere, like with inappropriate categories or an overly dry email sign-up process or an unlikeable love interest in the story itself.

There are two general types of Discovery Fail. One is obvious, and the other is difficult to spot until the damage has been done—and hard to fix even when you do realize what's happening.

Let's start super basic.

Books don't get magically discovered. It simply doesn't happen, sorry. As I said in my book *Let's Get Digital*, I don't believe in so-called "sleeper hits"—I think that's a lazy industry term, one which really means that we haven't figured out the reason for a given book's success. Of course, there can often be an element of luck in the planets seeming to align and a book really taking off into the stratosphere, and any kind of remarkable success is enough of an outlier to look a bit odd under the microscope. But you can often discern what primed the pump.

Readers, quite frankly, prefer hearing that a book's success was down to fate or cheesy serendipity or even plain old wonderful writing that simply muscled its way to the top. Publishers and agents and publicists (and authors) are often happy to feed that them that line. But it's usually fiction. The unvarnished truth is a little less Hollywood: there was a bit of sweat involved. Some hustle—or marketing, if you prefer.

Some authors seem to believe that if they just keep producing quality work, the world will eventually take notice. It doesn't work like that. If you are on my globally acclaimed mailing list, with its ever-so-helpful weekly tips and tricks, you would have heard these scary sounding numbers already. In case you are one of the few holdouts proving yet-resistant to my email charms: there are eight million ebooks in the Kindle Store—an imposing number on its own but a fraction of the 34 million-or-so titles in print right now, and let's not even mention the 100 million out-of-print books that can be borrowed from libraries or purchased from secondhand bookstores. Hey, it could be worse. You could be a blogger trying to get noticed among trillions of web pages!

I guess someone *could* somehow discover your work accidentally, buy it and love it, and then tell sufficient people who actually act on that recommendation in enough numbers—readers who, in turn, also happen to buy it, love it, and tell *still more people* until a groundswell of positive you-love sweeps the nation. But that's about as likely as spotting a needle hidden in one the haystacks of Idaho, from space, with Cylons on your tail that you just can't shake. Dammit, where's Starbuck…

Hey, it's good to prioritize new work. You should do that! But if you don't do anything to let readers know that it exists, that book will probably reach as many people as if you had left it gathering nanodust on your hard-drive.

This kind of Discovery Fail is trivial to spot: the author will have telephone number rankings, out in the millions, no one buying his work, no one even *seeing* his no-doubt-well-written books. Reviews and fan mail and Facebook likes and sell-through and email sign-ups are all generally a function of sales, so our hard-working author will be getting none of those either, and at this point he's probably feeling like it's all pointless and thinking of taking the toaster for a bath.

We've all been there. Luckily there are tons of things our erstwhile slogger can do to get eyeballs viewing his page, and I've already given you tons of examples of Discovery solutions in the earlier chapters about optimizing each stage, so I won't repeat myself here. Instead, I want to focus on the more insidious kind of Discovery Fail—where an author recognizes that he must pack away his beret for a moment and actually hustle with the rest of us to get some sales. But he doesn't have a good idea of his Ideal Reader and maybe also hasn't gotten a good handle on the kind of stuff he is writing, or who are solid comp authors, or any of that stuff.

He takes that first step of realizing he needs to actively market, he puts together a plan to bring readers to the Amazon page for his book and... it works? Sort of. He sells a little, I mean, and things seem to be moving, and he gets all excited, but things tail off very quickly. He notices some weird books creep into his Also Boughts, and a few months later, after sales tailing off completely and attempts at resuscitating them fail completely, the penny drops: he was targeting the wrong readers.

This is tricky, and more common than you might realize. I wrote a whole chapter earlier on the importance of granular targeting, but that was more focused on costs and optimization and the like. This is the other price you might pay for aiming outside your strict target audience: screwing up your Also Boughts.

Those who have read some of my other books will know this already, but it's important enough to bear repeating. Amazon's system will use your Also Boughts to determine which readers should be recommended your book. This is why you don't want Sue from Accounting who really prefers tentacle romance to buy your book. This is why you don't want Uncle Jem screwing up your Also Boughts with his tomes on historical sportsing. He and everyone else who isn't a genuine fan of your genre can buy later, when you have proper, relevant Also Boughts firmly attached. I don't care how long it takes—a day, a week, a month—you are better off selling nothing than selling to the wrong people.

That also goes for readers adjacent to your target market, by the way, which can trigger the worst kind of Discovery Fail of all, as it's the hardest to spot. You may have applied for BookBub Featured Deal and gotten accepted—but for a different list, one slightly outside your target market. You may have accepted anyway, and then sold reasonably well during the promotion, but then slightly inappropriate Also Boughts attached themselves like limpets to your book, forcing you into a death spiral with the Amazon recommendation engine.

This is a tough situation, and very tricky to solve—so tricky, in fact, that you must do your utmost to avoid it in the first place. Always make sure you know who your Ideal Readers are and that you are exclusively targeting them. As you'll see in the next chapters, that attitude must be applied not just to your ad choices, but into your presentation too—covers in particular.

# 18: Visibility Fail

A couple of years ago, I realized my life had gone full circle. This was around the time when it started to get noticeably harder to get accepted for a BookBub Featured Deal. It was never *easy*, as BookBub has the highest curatorial standards around—a big part of what makes it so popular with readers—but during 2016, if memory serves, I began putting more and more effort into pimping myself in that comment box on the application page. It would often go something like this:

> *Dear BB,*
>
> *I'm the very important author of this impeccably written book that's sold untold copies. I trust you will agree that featuring it would be an unparalleled treat for your readers. This promotion is part of a monster ad campaign that has the potential to realign the earth's magnetic field and I eagerly anticipate your excited acceptance letter.*
>
> *Kissylips,*
> *Dave*

Damn it, I was back to querying! BookBub's runaway popularity with power readers has made it the go-to promo site for authors. They are absolutely inundated with submissions and only have room to accept 20% of them, which makes it a tight squeeze when you are up against some of the biggest authors on the planet.

And just like querying agents, the process can make us a little potty, sometimes bleeding over into desperation—which is when we often make decisions we later regret. I'm speaking from experience here. I remember getting an acceptance from BookBub after several rejections, and I was so glad to get the *Yes* that I immediately dismissed concerns that it wasn't the category for which I had applied.

This is a fairly common situation for indies these days—they apply for one big, popular category, but get offered a smaller, newer category instead. For example, you might have applied for Contemporary Romance, which is a monster list costing $956 to get featured, but those books are sent out to an astonishing 2.25m subscribers, and usually result in 2,500 sales or more, covering that outlay immediately, and probably gate-crashing the Top 50 for good measure. However, it's also an insanely competitive category and authors can get shunted to a (somewhat) related category instead, like Chick Lit perhaps. That's much more competitively priced at $384, but the more muted results will reflect that lower price, and you might only get a third of the sales that the Contemporary Romance list might deliver.

However, that's not the big concern here. Our hypothetical romance author is a little concerned that her book isn't *quite* what you would strictly consider Chick Lit—she has a sassy protag and the book genuinely is funny, but while she might have some crossover with the likes of Jojo Moyes or Helen Fielding, she would never shelve her book beside theirs. She can see why BookBub might have suggested that category; the blurb and cover give off that vibe a little. Her book is sweeter than a lot of the steamy stuff dominating right now, and she had been aiming to convey that tone with her more chaste cover, but the style might be giving out some mixed messages to readers.

But she pushes that concern away. It's BookBub. There's a chance of huge sales here. She'd be foolish to pass that by, right? Maybe not. This kind of thing can go well, or badly, and when you see what happens when it goes well… you'll wish it went badly.

Let me explain. If you show your book cover to readers who are slightly outside your target market they'll either buy it, or not. If they don't buy it, you'll actually have dodged a bullet, and you can probably take comfort in the fact that your cover and blurb aren't attracting the wrong readers—just make a mental note to be stricter with your targeting next time. Sometimes no BookBub is better than any old BookBub.

But if these slightly-less-than-ideal readers *do* buy it, then the wrong Also Boughts will attach to your book. And if this happens during a BookBub promotion when you can get thousands of sales from readers outside your target market, then those Also Boughts will be extremely difficult to remove, and you're going to have a tough time on Amazon with that book; the system will recommend it to all the wrong readers any time you throw traffic at it, meaning any promo will have the dreaded dead cat bounce.

This lack of post-promo halo is one of the key signs of a Visibility Fail, but the cause of the fail can take many forms. Pointing the wrong kind of traffic at your book—solving a Discovery problem incorrectly, like with hitting the wrong category on BookBub—is just one kind of Visibility Fail. Others include choosing the wrong category for your books on Amazon, or inappropriate keywords (causing you to appear to the wrong readers in Amazon Search).

I spoke earlier in this book about how well-chosen categories and keywords can widen your visibility footprint on Amazon, adding an extra bounce to every promotion you run. This is true, but just like a Discovery problem, you can also solve a Visibility problem incorrectly. Any keywords or categories you apply to your book should be appropriate for that book's intended audience. If you start fooling yourself about the level of crossover appeal in your book (we all do it), then you can be guilty of overreach, and the next time you have a sales spike, and jump up the charts, you'll suddenly be visible to all the wrong readers—those browsing the Action/Adventure charts, instead of Historical Fiction, for example.

This is the exact same problem as being in a non-ideal BookBub category. Either these readers will ignore your book and you have wasted a visibility opportunity (i.e. you could have chosen alternative, more appropriate keywords and categories, and appeared to people who actually would like your book), or, even worse, they will buy it, and your Also Boughts will be polluted—to say nothing of potentially unhappy readers who could one-star your book on Amazon.

This is why every aspect of your book's presentation and metadata must ruthlessly target your Ideal Reader. Not only that, but you must be careful to avoid incorporating tropes from other genres in your cover and blurb. Your mystery set in Elizabethan London may have a strong romantic element, but if you choose to express that in your cover design too overtly, there is a danger that you may attract readers expecting an actual romance, i.e. one that obeys the conventions of the genre, such as a HEA. This can be a particular danger if you also focus on that couple in the blurb, or pair it with a title that could cause readers to double down on that wrong impression like *The Reluctant Prince*.

This is a common mistake. We might know we have written one kind of book for one type of reader, but when it comes to packaging that story or marketing it, we often worry that we might be limiting our audience by drilling down too much into that niche. Or we might be tempted to think we can tempt some readers from adjacent audiences. But if we look at books or authors that are true breakouts with crossover appeal, they usually started out targeting their niche quite ruthlessly. They learned to dominate their category first, and then parlayed that success into social proof for a broader audience. You even see publishers' ads being quite explicit about this, "If you read one thriller this year…"

So, work your niche first, then worry about being crowned Queen of All Things Written, because if you try to appeal to everyone from the get-go, you'll end up being a bland mush.

# 19: Consideration Fail

This is probably the easiest to spot. If you are successful in generating lots and lots of traffic towards your book's pages on Amazon, and it's the right kind of traffic, but nobody ends up buying your book, you probably have a classic Consideration Fail on your hands. That caveat— the right kind of traffic—is what distinguishes it from a Visibility Fail or Discovery Fail, and you must take some time to first establish whether that is indeed the case.

Again, the cause of a Consideration Fail is often down to a book's presentation, but rather than engaging too many of the wrong type of readers, your presentation isn't enticing anyone at all in your actual target market. A serious problem, no doubt, but one which has relatively straightforward solutions.

The key elements that convert a reader, once you have managed to get them to your product page, are as follows: author name, cover, price, blurb, reviews, sample. And they are probably more-or-less in that order of importance too. It's difficult to be exact here. Successive reader surveys show that the overwhelming reason that readers purchase a book is because they read something by the author before and enjoyed it. Hot on its tail is that the book was recommended by a trusted source, whether that was a teacher, newspaper review, or Amazon email—what is considered a trusted source is highly variable, of course.

Far in the distance, then, is everything else. However, that doesn't mean these conversion factors should be ignored. Quite the opposite. Your existing superfans won't care so much about the blurb or the cover or even the price—they are already hooked. I remember one author friend releasing Book 5 or 6 of an insanely popular series, and she was getting annoyed writing the blurb and just decided to go with "Oh you're going to buy it anyway." And they did.

These conversion factors assume huge importance for everyone who is not an existing superfan. Your most passionate readers might not care if your new release has a string of crappy reviews, but you better believe that will sway an on-the-fence purchaser. Same goes for the cover, the price, the sample, the title, and the blurb. Every single aspect of your presentation is a double-edged sword: an opportunity to close the sale, or something that might repel a potential purchaser.

If you think about it, you do this quite explicitly yourself. Often, you'll have your interest somewhat piqued by someone's recommendation and you'll check out a book. You look at the cover, read the blurb, then see it's $9.99 and decide to pass. Or you might see it's on sale and decide to grab it. Maybe you're the kind of browser who like to download the sample and let that be the tiebreaker, or you could prefer glancing at the reviews, hoping to be pushed over the edge, one way or the other.

The point is this: if all these potential conversion factors are in harmony, and appeal explicitly to your Ideal Reader, then your conversion rates will be excellent. You might notice that the huge authors in your category tend to have that almost intangible "bestseller" quality—that's what this is, all these elements in great shape: cover, blurb, reviews, title, sample, price all pulling in the same direction.

But if any of them are off, that can cause potential purchasers to pause. The more they hesitate, the greater the chance they will click away. Remember how many distractions are on your Amazon page? It's so easy to lose people, and readers aren't just looking for a reason to say yes, they are seeking to be swayed either way. The longer that process goes on without you closing the sale, the higher the chances they find something more intriguing in your Also Boughts.

And if your conversion rates are truly bad—i.e. if you

are sending lots of the right readers to your page and nobody is buying—then you might need a complete overhaul of your presentation. This is the bane of any marketer's life: lots of clicks and no sales. You've spent money on traffic, the campaign's targeting was great. Your CTRs were solid. Tons of your Ideal Readers poured into your Amazon pages and… bought something else.

It can be a giant pain in the ass to rework your presentation (blurbs especially). It can be expensive to commission a new cover. But until you do that, more traffic isn't going to solve this problem; it's just going to cost you more money. Worse than that, it's widely believed that Amazon factors conversion rates into its recommendation algorithms—a belief I share—so if you're sending thousands of people to your product page and they don't purchase, then the system won't be too keen on your book either.

Double fail.

# 20: Purchase Fail

This is where we lie to ourselves. The truth is too uncomfortable. No one wants to admit that they didn't land the storyplane. Instead, we insist internally that readers are busy. Overwhelmed with social engagements. They mustn't have had a chance to read *Magnum Opus* yet, or maybe they did and just forgot to review, and don't like signing up for newsletters. But they will surely pounce on *Magnum Opus II: the Embiggening* just as soon as they get a spare moment, and then gobble up the rest of the series too. Right?

If you have a sell-through problem, you have a product problem—which is a polite way of saying, while hiding all sharp objects from view, that there might be something wrong with the book. Nobody likes to hear that, of course. We get uncomfortable even considering the possibility. Writing is a unique kind of business, as we pour so much of *us* into our stories. I can't imagine the CEO of Colgate saying "FFS the new CoolFresh mouthwash is a flop, why does the world hate me? I'm such a terrible human being." But we do sometimes feel that way when our stories are criticized. It's personal in a way that other things aren't, and harder to shrug off. It gets much easier as you get more experience—that skin thickens into rhinohide!—but it never gets *easy*.

You must remind yourself of this: it's not personal. It doesn't mean that you're a subhuman piece of trash and you should break all your pens one by one and go live in the jungle. But maybe your big twist wasn't convincing. Perhaps your foreshadowing was a little *too* obvious and killed all the mystery. Or your star-crossed lovers didn't sizzle when they finally got it on. Somewhere along the line, you made a promise to the reader that you didn't keep. There are a million ways a story can feel off, as I'm sure you know. The hard part is admitting it to yourself. Easier to do when going through successive drafts, or getting criticism from betas, or heat from your editor. A bit harder to accept nine months down the road, when you've already done the big launch and all the related parping.

This is a Purchase Fail, and it *sucks*. You have been discovered by your Ideal Reader somewhere on Amazon or recommended by BookBub (or an actual human being). They went to your product page and navigated that minefield of Amazonian distraction and—Holy Buy Button, Batman—they actually bought your book. And then only read a page or two before tossing it aside. Damn it!

Of course, we don't have spy cameras in all our reader's houses (I believe Amazon isn't rolling that out until Q4, 2022). We can only deduce that readers didn't finish our book by looking at a subpar sell-through percentage, paired with other absent indicators like a surprisingly low number of reviews, or lack of sign-ups, or fan mail. Or we can more directly know that's the case by getting a load of stinky reviews, complete with that three-pronged scarlet letter: DNF.

This is a crappy problem to wrestle with, and may require some tough self-talk. Or whiskey. Whatever works. Once you accept you have a problem (which you must do, so you don't continue to waste time and energy and headspace wondering why all those marketing dollars are moving Book 1 but not Book 2), then you have a tough decision to make. This is a real bear. Do you go back and fix the book, or do you cut it loose and move on?

It depends. There's probably only one of my novels that I wouldn't start hacking away at if the manuscript was put in front of me—but that's perfectly natural. If you are not improving with each book, you mustn't be pushing yourself enough. But that doesn't mean I will go back and rewrite them all, for that way lies madness. Speaking to authors who have attempted this, it can be an endless rabbit hole of frustration and negativity. And for what? Shouldn't that energy be spent creating something new?

That argument holds up pretty well when you're just talking about standalones. (However, if you're selling a collection of standalones, then you might have a different problem altogether—one of strategy, because it's considerably easier to make money and build audience with a series or something that you can more-or-less market as a series to readers, such as books that are connected in some way or another.) But when you're talking about a series, the rationale for doing that remedial work can be stronger.

I know authors who have gone back and fixed Book 1 to bring it up closer to the level of subsequent installments. There are still dangers here, as it's generally better to move forward rather than backward, but this makes a little more sense—especially if it's a permafree or otherwise getting pushed to a broader audience.

These considerations aside—and only you will know the right answer—the most important thing to do with these reader satisfaction principles is to internalize them and make sure subsequent work avoids these pitfalls. Like most authors, I'm always working on my craft in one way or another, either explicitly on a certain aspect or technique, or implicitly by simply writing. When not admiring my ever-expanding collection of Fabergé eggs, that is.

Okay. Now that we have tiptoed across the wafer-thin ice of shoddy writing, let's move on to a subject that won't be touchy at all: how terribly you treat people!

# 21: Advocacy Fail

It's a classic error: thinking your job is over once the cash register rings. That sweet, sweet sound can dull our senses, leading us to think we are at the end of our relationship with that customer, when really you should be moving to second base. This isn't the end of anything: it's the beginning of something else, something much more beautiful—repeat business.

We think our wordspells will be enough to bewitch readers, and sometimes they are, but here's where it's really important to put yourself in the shoes of your Ideal Reader. Remember her? The soccer mom with three young kids who still works from home three days a week in her well-paid, but highly stressful, public relations gig? The one who treats her reading time as sacred, as it's the one part of her day she can (sometimes!) switch off and not get asked forty-seven questions about whether dogs get sad.

When she's not Googling ways of removing chewing gum from hamster fur, she likes to escape with romantic suspense. Yes, she bought your book, and was looking forward to the sequel, but she's also a huge fan of Cristin Harber and JD Robb, who are no slouches. Those authors are insta-buys for her, and she could miss your upcoming release in the excitement of seeing a new *Titan* or *In Death* book. Maybe she had previously clicked on your mailing list sign-up link but found the process overly complicated... and then was distracted by her kids trying to give Mr. Pickles a bath on the living room floor.

This kind of thing happens every day.

If sales are good, then you're not in bad shape. Your Ideal Readers are making it through four of five stages without major issues, or at least in sufficient numbers to keep you afloat. But if you have mailing list envy when your author-peers are talking about how much money they fork out to Mailchimp every month, then you might have an Advocacy Fail. If you never seem to have the same crazy passionate fans as others in your niche, despite outselling them, this is a clear sign that you have an issue at this stage. which is okay—this is the trickiest part!

Some authors are total naturals at this; they're the ones with the outsized lines at their con table, the ones whose fans get quotes tattooed on their midriff, or name kids after characters in their books, or buy limited edition signed hardbacks, or mugs, or any kind of merch related to the book. They might have tons more Facebook Likes than you—or the same amount of followers but much more engaged ones, who seem to comment and share every post, and make each new release announcement go viral. These are the ones who have insanely passionate responses to their launch emails, seeming to hit the Top 100 on Amazon without breaking a sweat. You can get there too, but it seems to require a bigger push, more effort, a larger outlay. They make it seem… effortless.

It's anything but. However, the hard work was put in a long time before today. They have built this relationship over time, and they're reaping the rewards now. If you are the opposite—if you feel like you're starting from near-zero with each release; if you have the growing, uncomfortable sense that your readership has plateaued, despite your production levels rising and your marketing spend increasing; if you see authors with fewer books and few miles on the clock leapfrogging you inexplicably; if your mailing list is far smaller than it should be or, even more dangerous, deteriorating in responsiveness with each release—then it's quite likely that you have an Advocacy Fail.

Hey, at least you only have one stage to optimize. The solutions have a lot of moving parts, no doubt, and require an ongoing time investment—probably the last thing a busy author wants to hear—and perhaps also a mindset shift. But it *is* doable.

And the sooner you grapple with it, the less painful it will be.

# PART V

## SOLVE IN REVERSE

You know your Ideal Readers now, the five stages they pass through on their journey from strangers to super-fans, the blockages that can create a fail *and* how to fix each stage so that you have the most optimal Reader Journey. You have the ability now to dive in to fix things efficiently, but what if there's a book or series that demands a complete top-to-tail makeover? Don't worry; I have you covered: just make sure to solve in reverse. This final section will show you how, while also serving as a handy refresher for the entire book. How serendipitous!

# 22: Why We Work Backwards

If you have the time, money, inclination, or overarching need, and wish to renovate every aspect of a series, it's incredibly important to know in which order you must tackle these tasks. This process takes time, especially if you're sprucing up every aspect of an extensive back catalogue—which I've done!—and if you solve your Discovery or Visibility issues before tackling Purchase or Advocacy problems then you are just funneling more people into a broken system. If you want to build a fully functioning Superfan Factory, you should solve in reverse.

I recommend splitting up your remodeling tasks into three broad groups: Product, Presentation, and Promotion. The first group deals with Purchase and Advocacy issues. The second will handle Consideration and Visibility matters. And the third will focus exclusively on Discovery solutions. In other words, you should fix conversion at each stage before pumping up the traffic, and it makes the most sense to work backwards.

I'll walk through each set of tasks in successive chapters, which will also act as a handy summary of all the methods and approaches in this book. But to give you a general idea first: your Product analysis will look at the book itself—both the story and its front and end matter—as well as how you treat those readers after you capture them (or how to address not capturing them at all!). Presentation will look at the entire package being presented to readers: cover, description, price, and metadata such as keywords and categories. Then, and only then, do I suggest moving on to Promotion, and the various strategies for pumping up traffic.

All the other stuff must be slick first, or you simply won't get the necessary return on that spend. It's great to design a winning onboarding sequence that will encourage more readers to sign up to your list and become long-term, engaged subscribers who open every email and purchase every new release on launch day. But it's much smarter to have that in place *before* you invest money in a big advertising campaign designed to ramp up sales, rather than scrambling afterwards.

# 23: The Product

They say you should never get high on your own supply. Probably good advice, but you need to assume the mantle of your Ideal Reader now and take a good hard look at what you're selling them. We'll look at the presentation in the next chapter, but first you need to examine what's inside the package:

## Book

Is there anything more annoying than Smug Successful Author being asked the secret of his success and him replying, "it's really all about having a great story." And here was me writing mediocre trash like an idiot all this time! A good book might be a necessary for success but it's most certainly not sufficient—and some might argue the first part, while side-eying the charts. I'll assume you are all professionals who take pride in putting out a good product. Looking at the book itself must still form part of your review though. Maybe it's a standalone that can't be repackaged or marketed as anything series-like, and you have to maybe consider if it's worth putting marketing behind, whether you'll get the results you want, or if the book is better deployed as a reader magnet, perhaps. It could be the case that it's a Book 1 of the very first series you wrote, and could conceivably benefit from a more rigorous editor this time around, or even another pass. One of the most successful authors I know ended up going back to do another draft of his very first book when it ended up being the opener of a hugely successful series. He could see some drop off between Books 1 and 2 that indicated an issue and he gritted his teeth and rectified it, unpalatable as the task initially seemed. And it worked too.

## End Matter

Your end matter should be clean, clear, and compelling. While your needs may vary a touch from book-to-book and series-to-series, a good general approach is to think about which book is most logical for readers to move to next. That's pretty obvious at the end of Book 2, but maybe less so at the end of a given series. Try and usher them towards something else, just don't try and flog them *everything* else right now. Pick one book, drop in an enticing sentence and a clickable link, then move on to your mailing list push, review request, and social media/website links. If you have tons of books, consider *not* including them all. Just a link to your site or your

Amazon author page is fine, or perhaps mentioning a spin off series if they have just concluded the main one. I think readers can be overwhelmed sometimes when they see an author has 25 more books, especially if she just lists them all out without indicating where to go next. Make sure all this is the *very first thing* readers see after The End. Acknowledgements, Author's Note, Dedication, whatever other stuff you have in your end matter (and these days I minimize all that as much as possible), put that after all of your reader requests, or else they may not get seen at all, let alone acted upon.

## Email Sign-up Process & Newsletter Best Practices

Not strictly inside the package you're selling readers, but it is the very first place you will want them to visit once they're done reading, aside from a link to the next book in the series. What happens when readers click that sign-up link in your end matter? Do they get taken to a cold, generic sign-up page with boilerplate? Or do they see a customized page with branded series graphics and enticing language explaining what *they* get for signing up? Do you only email them when you have a new book (i.e. when you want something from them)? Or do you deliver value to them regularly? Do you fail to communicate with them after they sign up? Or do you nurture the relationship right from the start with an optimized automation sequence that welcomes them to your list and trains them to open your emails by delighting them with relevant content?

## Platform

Are you present where your readers are? Do you link to that presence in your end matter? And do you follow through on that implicit promise by being active on those platforms and sharing content they enjoy? Remember, I'm not suggesting you need to spend half your time posting memes on Facebook or artfully presented croissants on Instagram, their buttery deliciousness notwithstanding.

If you only have the time or inclination to communicate with readers through one channel, I suggest you make that email. Facebook is next in order of priority, purely because that's where almost everyone's readers are, and it's also the biggest advertising platform—one which is much easier to get benefit from if you already have a thriving Facebook Page.

But if you have the time, or overarching reader need, you can add another layer or two to your social media presence. Just make sure to have, at least, a basic website where anyone can find information about your books and where to purchase them. The pressure to have an all-conquering author platform can be overwhelming—but I think it's overstated too. Employing email best practices, having an active Facebook Page, and building a basic website will get you very far indeed.

Once you have addressed all the issues with your product, and the places we drive readers towards after they hit *The End*, it's time to look at… your package.

# 24: The Presentation

Repeat after me: a cover isn't an art project; it's commercial packaging for a product. And the cover is just the most visceral part, the aspect readers are more likely to encounter first. You also need to consider everything else too: the blurb, title, subtitle (for non-fiction in particular), price, and sample. And, hey, while we're at it, your author bio. Say what?

## Cover

First impressions are key, and your cover is what your Ideal Reader will likely encounter first, often at thumbnail size in a sea of other covers—either in Amazon search results, or in the Also Boughts of another book, or in a deals newsletter like BookBub. Your designer doesn't think that way. They have a 260-inch 10k Super Retina display, and those subtle little touches they spent time layering onto your ornate cover are going to look like a blurry smudge when the tech-philistines at the ebookstore shrink this work of art down to the size of a desktop icon.

## Blurb

The blurb is important, but the first three or four lines are crucial. That's all that will appear "above the fold." Amazon now truncates anything more than that, and readers must actively click to see the rest. You would think a description of the book is more important than an ad for someone else's—or an ad for shirts, which is what is currently on the page for my novel *Liberty Boy*. Amazon views this differently, so we have to navigate this challenge.

In short, make the blurb hooky as hell and, most importantly, open with a bang. If you have some stellar social proof (like that you're a *New York Times* bestseller), you'd better not bury it! This is sales copy, not a book report, which I'm sure you know. Just make sure not to dial up the hype too much either. It should still be written in your voice—that's what your Ideal Reader will respond to most of all.

## Price

Pretty easy. Price like the bestsellers in your niche. The indie bestsellers, I mean. Ignore those crazy-ass traditional publishers; they are playing a different game completely (protecting the print market).

## Sample

The book is already in great shape, so the sample should be also. Just check that your sample is opening in the right place, ensure that all that extraneous front matter is moved to the back (or dispensed with completely), and make sure you capture reader attention instantly.

## Author Bio

You might think this is nuts, but hear me out. Remember how little real estate you control on your Amazon product page? The Author Bio might not be the most visible of that, but it's one crucial little island you have power over. The savviest authors are already using this as another conversion element. I don't mean by dropping in some salesy crap, but by cleverly writing this text in their natural authorial voice, i.e. in such a way that it appeals to their Ideal Reader. I think mine is (finally) in pretty good shape but go look at the one for CD Reiss if you want to see someone who is effortlessly good at this. Remember this text box will also pop up on Amazon Search so make sure the first line or two has a hook—just like a blurb. And all this goes double for non-fiction, where the experience or qualifications are more important for readers. Even voice sometimes, for a dry topic. If I have to read a book on taxes, I don't want the teacher from—anyone, anyone?—Ferris Bueller narrating it.

# 25: The Promotion

Finally! Your book is in wonderful shape, delighting readers from first to last, and your end matter is leveraging that reader-love into cold, hard email addresses. These readers will then be regaled with further stellar content that will nurture them into superfans—not an overnight process of course, but you have the processes in place now to encourage this transformation. Your presentation is *slick* too. Not just a killer cover and buy-me-now blurb, but excellent metadata best practices have been deployed, so your book can be visible to as many of your Ideal Readers as possible, without appealing/appearing to too many of the wrong ones.

Ready for your close-up, in other words. Let's turn up the juice.

## Promo Strategies for Amazon-Exclusive Authors

This type of plan will work best for a Kindle Unlimited author, but don't skip this if you have wider distribution—there's stuff in here you can apply to your books too. You will be selling on Amazon whether you are wide or exclusive; it's just that exclusive authors can afford to be a little more aggressive with price and advertising spend when they are in KDP Select, because they get all those borrows on top of sales, and 70% on Countdown deals regardless of price, doubling the return on investment for 99¢ promos. Both of these factors will bring extra ad revenues (and saucier CPCs) into play for the Countdown-using Kindle Unlimited author.

Success in Kindle Unlimited comes down to one thing: visibility. It was always important to chase visibility on Amazon, because appearing to lots of new eyeballs in the charts will turn into sales (caveat: some charts are more well-trafficked by readers than others). Much more importantly however, sales and rank and visibility are what trigger wide-scale recommendations by Amazon—both on the site itself, and in the millions of emails Amazon sends out every day to customers. When you see a book mysteriously getting "sticky" in the charts, this algorithmic glue is usually what's behind it.

That visibility is worth significantly more to exclusive authors. Kindle Unlimited subscribers see a different Amazon—one that is split into free books they can borrow at will, and one where the books cost money. Which do you think they will prefer?

They also have different recommendation pathways. Amazon has entirely separate algorithms for deciding which books they get recommended. There's nothing particularly nefarious about this. If these are the books Kindle Unlimited subscribers will prefer, then these are the types of books Amazon's system will defer towards when recommending reads.

I go into some detail in my free book *Amazon Decoded* about how all this works, but all you really need to know is that visibility is gold if you are exclusive, and your marketing should be built around attaining it, and holding on to it for as long as possible. This generally means you can be much more aggressive with your marketing spend, and even price too. When I'm running big Kindle Unlimited campaigns, I will make deeper price cuts, and leave those prices lower for longer. I'm always confident I'll make the money back—and then some—in a page read wave that will kick in a week or so after the campaign.

Kindle Unlimited rewards big, bold campaigns. Unlike when you have wider distribution, and you tend to spread your marketing around, exclusive authors should concentrate their firepower. I often advertise hard for five-to-seven days and then coast for the rest of the month—and that can often be enough to sustain considerable page reads per day until it is time for the next campaign. In the next chapter, you'll see just how many reads this kind of approach can generate.

## Promo Strategies for Wide Authors

There's no point crying about Kindle Unlimited-powered books pushing you down every hour, adding up to a visibility blockade; it is what it is. Focus on your advantages. The first is that you can get sales anywhere. It doesn't matter to you if a sale comes in from Apple Australia or Kobo Canada; it's all money. Readers there are cheaper to reach and are much more deal starved. Retailers like Apple, Barnes & Noble, and Kobo lean heavily towards expensive traditionally published books. This is an opportunity for you.

You will notice right away that your ad campaigns on BookBub will have much more impressive CTRs when you target readers internationally and outside Amazon. Impressions are cheaper as there's less competition for those eyeballs. Readers are more responsive to a free offer or heavily discounted book, because they simply have fewer of those to choose from outside America and outside Amazon. Books are incredibly expensive in countries like Australia. The market there, and in Canada, and in the United Kingdom, is not serviced to anything like the same level. Contrast that with all the deal sites that have flooded the American market. Additionally, most of those deal sites only serve Kindle owners. The average British Kobo customer, for example, does not experience anything like the same amount of deals as a user of the US Kindle Store.

Which means they respond much better to them. I particularly recommend using CPM bidding in BookBub Ads for this purpose. CPC bidding might be more familiar to you, but CPM has two key advantages: first, if your ads are in great shape those clicks work out cheaper; second, they are much better at teaching you best practices. If you are running CPM ads your overarching focus will be on optimizing CTR, and each improvement on that percentage will both reduce your click costs and extend your audience—as you burn through it at a slower rate.

BookBub also has some very tidy options for running micro-targeting campaigns. If you want to reach just Apple users in Canada, you can do so. This means you can go wherever clicks are cheapest, instead of engaging in the Thunderdome that can be the American market. I'm writing a historical novel set in Australia. It's great to know I'll be able to swamp that starved market with ads and reach that built-in audience very cheaply indeed. There are a lot of Apple users in Australia, and I don't have that market closed to me. I can cover the whole market with one easy-to-make ad.

I can do that on Facebook too, of course, it's just not always as straightforward and requires quite a bit of experimentation—which can cost you until you reach a good level of optimization. The other problem with Facebook and a market like Australia is that my ads will serve mostly to people who still read print books, whereas BookBub is all readers who have gone digital. (Yes, I could filter that Facebook audience by ebook consumers, but Facebook isn't very good at identifying them.)

You don't have the cream of borrows on top of your sales, visibility on Amazon is worth a little less to you than it is to a Kindle Unlimited author, and you get half the royalties at 99¢. Which means everything else has to work harder: your website, your mailing list, your deal sites. You can and should be more aggressive about building up your lists. You need to use BookBub Ads to run micro-targeting campaigns and find the cheapest clicks, wherever they may be. And you have the killer advantage of being much more likely to get accepted for a BookBub Featured Deal.

Permafree is available to you in a way that it isn't for exclusive authors. You have more flexibility with reader magnets, as you don't have to worry about exclusivity. Embrace all the things you can do and try to forget about what's out of reach. I know plenty of authors who are killing it with wide distribution, and they all have a similar enough approach: they don't chase rank and visibility the way Kindle Unlimited authors do. They don't have that overarching focus on the US Kindle Store. They don't need to make that big splash. Instead they take a drip marketing approach, creating many possible streams of sales that all combine into a fine total.

# 26: The Superfan Factory

Welcome to your new office. This is your command center, where you will oversee the transformation of your back catalog into a machine that converts at every stage of the Reader Journey. I like to call it The Superfan Factory.

There has been a lot of information in this book that is either conceptual or intangible—such is the nature of the topic, and our business in general too. But I'd like to close this book with something very hands-on indeed: an actual case study of how all these principles were put into practice, and the remarkable results this approach can generate. Before we dive into that, though, I want to quickly recommend a few tools to help you track those sales/ranks and generally analyze performance—the supervillain dashboard for your Superfan Factory.

The best tool for tracking ranks on Amazon is a free one called eBookTracker. This covers the US Kindle Store only, but does so in great depth, allowing you to see rank movements over the last 24 hours, 30 days, or full year. It also tracks price changes and can even keep tracking a book when it switches from paid to free, and vice versa, something that can break similar tools. It's also much more customizable than others of this ilk. You can make groups of books—handy for viewing all of yours in one place, or just tracking a single series (of your own, or another author). Glitches are few and far between too, meaning the data is almost always reliable. It works from the Amazon API, so it should be up-to-date—usually capturing a rank change about an hour after it actually happens on the Kindle Store.

No such rank-tracking tools exist for the other retailers (App Annie used to do a great job of tracking Apple, but that aspect of their service was nixed, unfortunately), but then Amazon is probably going to be the majority of your sales anyway, even if you opt for wider distribution.

Tracking those sales is a bit of a mixed bag. KDP reports are much better than they were, but they still fall short in some areas, leading authors to explore third-party tools like Book Report—free until you start earning $1,000 a month, from which point it costs $19 a month. This is significantly more than the $10 a month it used to cost, so you'll have to weigh up yourself whether it is worth it, if you fall into that bracket. I personally decided to stop paying for it not long after that price hike and can no longer recommend it with the same gusto as before.

Book Report has added new features for Kindle Un-limited that might make it more desirable to exclusive authors, but it never did roll out the ability to capture non-Amazon retailers that was openly mooted at the time of that price hike. Indeed, many of the much-trumpeted new features seem to have been implemented with uncharacteristic sloppiness and reports of negative customer service experiences have risen. Keep all that in mind, but if you are just starting out you can try it for free.

Doing an admirable job of handling all the different-ly formatted reports and spreadsheets coming from all the various ebook retailers is Trackerbox. It's a little easier to recommend this tool without caveats as it costs a flat fee ($89.99) and has a 45-day free trial too. The software is regularly updated, with a much-requested Mac version just about to be launched. Because it's a downloadable software program, rather than something that lives in your browser like Book Report, you must manually feed it your monthly reports and the visuals aren't as pretty, but you can do all sorts of analysis and spit out various summaries that could be very useful for your accountant. It can also handle reports for audio sales, paperbacks, even books you might hand-sell at a convention. Nothing else out there is as comprehensive; just don't expect it to do the same kind of one-click, on-the-fly analysis as Book Report.

One popular alternative to both TrackerBox and BookReport is BookTrakr—but I'm personally wary of any tool that requires such access to your Amazon account (and all the other retailers also), so I haven't tried it. If that's not a concern for you, go for it, but I recommend avoiding another alternative called AKReport, which has had security issues in the past, as well as questions about who is running it and what they are doing with the data collected.

Moving away from sales and rank tracking, PrettyLinks is a free plug-in for WordPress that acts both as a customizable link shortener for your own domain, and also a link redirecter. Very handy for tidying things up. And, finally, I just want to briefly mention ReaderLinks. I don't use it personally, so I won't go into great detail, but it's quite an ambitious tool which aims to help you organize your street team, measure the ROI on your ads, and a dozen other things too. ReaderLinks wasn't for me, but it might be for you. Links to all these tools, and more, will be on the Resources page for this book at *DavidGaughran.com/SuperfansResources*. I do keep that page updated as well.

Okay, let's ditch this bunch of tools; it's time to jump into the hot tub of outrageous success.

## Building An Army of Superfans: A Case Study

I worked with science fiction author Jay Allan for a couple of years as a marketing consultant. I don't do that kind of work anymore, in case anyone asks, but thought it would be a good idea to share some of that experience with you (with Jay's kind permission) and show you exactly how these principles work in practice.

A friend of mine—Phoenix Sullivan—had been helping Jay with some launches, so he could spend more time writing his insanely popular books, and she suggested my name when stepping aside to focus on her own work. I was intrigued by working with such a big author and also putting into play some strategies I'd been sketching out for a while—and the opportunity to do that across an extensive catalog if books in a popular niche was very attractive indeed. Jay was completely open to trying anything, so it sounded like a very fun project. And the results have been ridiculous, which is also fun!

The headline numbers are going to blow you away, so it's crucial to register a couple of immediate caveats in case anybody gets the wrong impression. First, taking over from a genius like Phoenix Sullivan is like finishing off an interior decorating job where Michelangelo has already done the ceiling; I just had to keep going along the same lines. Second, Jay was already an incredibly popular author with ridiculously devoted fans (I mean, seriously), a large mailing list, a lot of connections and cross-promo opportunities, a recognizable name in his genre, a *USA Today* Bestseller, a huge back catalog, an impressive release schedule, enough sales to sustain a healthy marketing budget... you get the idea. I wasn't starting from zero here. Jay was also game enough to pretty much give me free rein on the marketing side, which was an incredible amount of trust from Day One.

The results went some way towards repaying that leap of faith, I think. Over the eighteen months, or so, that we worked together, Jay received a Kindle Unlimited All Star Bonus every single month—bar one, if I remember right, when we had to delay a launch and cancel the associated promo. For those unaware, the floor to get a Kindle All Star Bonus in the US was just over 4m page reads at the time (it's a little higher now). I should also mention that Phoenix had already garnered Jay a few of those before I came along, so keep that in mind, along with all the other caveats above. By the time we finished working together, though, Jay was pulling in well over 10 million page reads a month, which was pretty incredible.

How did we put together the kind of marketing campaigns that generate those numbers? I mean, aside from the gold-plated head-start? By adopting the principles I've spoken about throughout this book. But we had to be systematic about it. There were over thirty titles in Jay's catalog, so doing everything at once would have been impossible even with a team of ten; perhaps the way we attacked it will help guide your efforts if you have a lot of titles yourself.

First, we took a look at the product itself. The overwhelmingly positive reviews and already-existing passionate fanbase meant we could be confident the books themselves were in great shape, which meant there was only a little work to be done on the front and end matter to bring it into line with current best practices and achieve some consistency across the catalog.

Unless there are specific needs in mind, I generally like to be very explicit about which title you are pushing readers towards next in your end matter, and have that (along with email capture) be the very first thing readers see and the main focus. For example, rather than simply present readers with an organized list of 30+ titles, I wanted to have a direct, clickable link for Book 2 be one of the first things readers are presented with at the end of Book 1—in their face, if you like.

Regarding presentation, there was a little work to do in terms of cover refreshes. Obviously, with 30+ titles, if you are talking about brand new covers for everything, that is a considerable amount of money, and you will be waiting a long time for the work to be done (or you'll have to source several designers simultaneously, which is far from ideal). Given that one series already had excellent illustrations, we felt we could get pretty far on the older books with a little retouching and some quality re-lettering—which had the side-benefit of greatly reducing both the cost and the time it took to get the work done.

When it came to metadata, we reviewed pretty much the entire catalog, ensuring his visibility footprint was as wide as possible and that he was appearing to all segments of his target readership, while being careful not to spill over into inappropriate categories. We further optimized the keywords to increase his search footprint too, and again to achieve some consistency in each series, so all nine books of a given series would all appear on the same search terms, giving a heavy blast of social proof when paired with all the amazing reviews the books had already garnered from loyal fans.

Then it was time to turn up the traffic. Jay was pretty much all-in with Kindle Unlimited, which meant we could be aggressive with both pricing and advertising. We ran a series of multi-pronged campaigns, usually one a month where we would advertise heavily for five-to-seven days and then just coast off that for the rest of the month. This isn't a book about advertising or algorithms, but there is more information on that approach to marketing on the Resources page for this book at *DavidGaughran.com/SuperfansResources*.

In short, we threw everything at these books we could think of, confident now that we would optimize greater numbers of readers at each stage of The Reader Journey and get a much better return from the money Jay was investing in marketing. We did free runs and Countdown deals, often in combination across a whole series. We pushed the discounts on deal sites. Facebook and BookBub Ads became increasingly important with each campaign, as we refined targeting and could identify Jay's Ideal Readers more readily. Deal sites are often the cheapest clicks out there, and the best place to dangle a freebie to brand-new readers, for example, but they don't scale to the level we needed.

BookBub Ads is a great platform—super responsive, wonderful targeting. You have to burn through a little money to figure out your targeting, and what kind of images your Ideal Readers respond to, but once you do you are set, and every campaign can be as successful as the last, with minor refinements. This is an island of consistency in a world of variables, and truly invaluable.

Facebook is a little wonkier all round, but there is one area where it destroys the competition: scale. If you can develop your own custom audiences on Facebook— large pools of your Ideal Readers—that really is the golden goose. Again, it takes a fair bit of experimentation and patience, but you can slowly do this over time.

With deal sites, BookBub Ads, Facebook, newsletter swaps, email blasts, and price promotions, we built a machine that turbocharged Jay's Kindle Unlimited page reads and took his readership to new heights.

But here's the thing: we wouldn't have gotten anything like the same return if we hadn't done the less glamorous work behind the scenes first. It was quite a job, revamping that catalog. These books were already selling, so wasn't like we could pull a series down while we refurbished it. Everything had to be done on the fly, but we just took it one series at a time and gave priority to whichever "universe" had a book coming out next. It took some time to go through it all, but the cumulative results were spectacular.

These principles apply whether you are already a big seller or still in the initial stages of building your audience. Equally to fiction and non-fiction, by the way, as you will see from my own experience when I took a similar approach to relaunching my own career. In my case, I work in two very different genres, ones where organic crossover is so low that I actually need to build walls between my readerships to prevent things like Also Bought pollution and reader confusion and a big mess on the branding front.

Let me give you the breakdown on how that revamp went—on the non-fiction side, in particular. After years of handling all this the wrong way, I had: a mixed list of fiction and non-fiction—people just lumped together; a website trying to serve both kinds of books, and not doing a very good job with either; and a Facebook Page where I was mostly followed by writers—as that was the content I tended to post more frequently—along with a handful of very confused, and critically disengaged fiction readers. This unholy mess began to impact sales also, particularly on the fiction side where my Also Boughts were getting swamped by non-fiction books. None of this was good, of course, so it required a serious rework.

This was a big job and the immediate priority was sorted out the mailing list, and also the non-fiction side of my business in general, as I had impending releases. First, I split my mailing list in two, and tried to shepherd my fiction readers onto a new, dedicated list. I also did the same with my website and my Facebook Page— creating dedicated spaces with content specific to those readers—and subsequently relaunched my fiction under a slightly tweaked author name (and my Also Boughts improved overnight). But email was the most urgent, so I tackled that first.

Knowing that my list was now exclusively made up

of writers was immediately liberating, and I began a weekly newsletter sharing tips and tricks every Friday, helping authors learn more about things like BookBub Ads or how to optimize their Amazon categories. I also set up a neat little onboarding sequence to welcome new people to my list, talking about things like effective cover design, book discoverability, and reader targeting. While this is a pretty basic example of an automated sequence, it still accomplished a number of tasks at once. It trained people to expect an email from me at regular intervals, helped those messages actually reach their inboxes, (diplomatically) weeded out the freeloaders who just wanted the free book, and built up engagement by feeding them evergreen examples of the kind of "live" content that would be arriving each week when they completed the welcome sequence and joined the main list.

I've since changed that welcome sequence for a number of reasons—primarily because my non-fiction list became so well known that people were demanding to get to the "live" content quicker, just in case you do sign up to take a gander at it. But it did its job for that first year, as you will see in a moment.

Something that really helped boost those numbers funneling through that initial welcome sequence was writing an exclusive reader magnet. This is where you start harvesting serious benefits from having a strong idea of your Ideal Reader—putting yourself in their shoes and really thinking deeply about what kind of content they would value most, coming up with something truly desirable which people only get if they sign up to your list. It worked a treat; my list doubled in the space of a few weeks and was up 600% within a year.

It wasn't just sign-ups which exploded. Engagement soared also, helped along by giving that freebie to all my existing subscribers as a sweetener for sticking around after the switch to a weekly newsletter format, but also by prioritizing my list. Treating sign-ups with respect. Being super focused on delivering value. Ensuring that there were a number of enticing benefits to subscribing so that the whole operation began to feel like an exclusive club that people *really wanted to join*, rather than a simple newsletter. All of this resulted in a large increase in opens, clicks, subscriber numbers, and positive feedback also.

This approach might be a little more work than simply emailing people about new releases (perhaps less than you might think?), but I actually found it invigorating at a time when I'd become a little burned out. Now, some of you may be aghast at the idea of hitting your list every week, but don't worry. I only email my fiction list monthly, and that's enough for that crowd, and probably for most authors. The right system for you will depend on all sorts of things, but the aim is always the same: to deliver value and increase engagement. The *how* will vary quite a lot depending on you and your readers.

There were a lot of other things I overhauled about my non-fiction business. I improved my branding, my targeting, the quality of the graphics I was using both as headers on my social media profiles and in my ads. Something like content marketing might be more important for a non-fiction author than advertising but having consistent branding which appeals to your Ideal Reader is important whatever path you take to them. Everything was pulling in the right direction for once, and the overall effect on sales and income was spectacular. And once all that was up and running, I started tackling my fiction business, restructuring my catalog, offering a new reader magnet, tweaking my welcome sequence until the numbers were healthy, boosting sign-ups, rolling out monthly engaging content—all with my Ideal Reader in mind. I now have a brand new list of happy and engaged readers who are eager for my next release… which makes the writing side a lot more enjoyable too.

I hope these two examples give *you* the confidence that these methods work. And I look forward to hearing how you all get on.

See you at the top of the charts!

# About The Author

David Gaughran was born in Ireland but now lives in a quaint little fishing village in Portugal, although this doesn't seem to have increased the time he spends outside. He writes historical fiction and science fiction under another name, has helped tens of thousands of authors publish their work and build a career for themselves through his workshops, blog, and writers' books—*Let's Get Digital, Strangers to Superfans, Amazon Decoded, BookBub Ads Expert*, and *Following*—and has also created giant marketing campaigns for some of the biggest self-publishers on the planet.

If you enjoyed *Strangers to Superfans*, David would greatly appreciate a review online. Even a word or two would be more helpful than you know.

In case you are wondering which of his many books for authors to read next, David recommends *BookBub Ads Expert: A Marketing Guide to Author Discovery*—which manages to be both a comprehensive guide to the world's hottest book advertising platform, and also the funniest book David has written. Rumors abound that he wrote it in the pub, which he is yet to deny. But if you would prefer more hands-on help to find your first readers, David suggests signing up to his free course *Starting from Zero*—which you can find at *David Gaughran.com*.

David also sends out weekly tips and tricks to over ten thousand authors every Friday, as you may have guessed from frequent nudges and accompanying winks. If you want free marketing advice every week, make sure to sign up to his list (and grab your free book!) at *DavidGaughran.com*.

Finally, please feel free to follow him on Twitter, get in touch on Facebook, watch his YouTube channel to check the progress on his beard, or just send him an email. He will answer you personally... which may be a pro or a con. You can find links to all those places, and a contact form, at the above website.

# Author Note

I had to pull together a new production team for this book and they have all been wonderful—fast, professional, quality work. Flexible too, understanding of my demanding schedule as we published three titles in twelve weeks and I kept doing that thing where I didn't finish the writing in time.

Tammi Labrecque did a stellar job with the edits, Alexios Saskalidis came up with a striking cover design for quite an ethereal topic, and Michelle Hart jumped on the proofreading grenade when I was in big trouble. Thank you all.

This book would never have been possible without the openness of self-publishers to share what's working for them; I'd like to thank Jay Allan in particular for allowing me to talk about some of his results. Also, Andrew Rhomberg at Jellybooks was kind enough to share information with me about his company's reader analytics experiments. Ernie Dempsey and countless other writers let me bug them incessantly about the different things they are doing to build an army of passionate readers. And Kit Rocha was especially generous with her time and knowledge, particularly her instinctive ability to weave reader catnip throughout her stories and marketing messages.

While these three books were published in just over three months, I have been working on the concepts and testing theories behind them for a year. Throughout that time Ivča has been incredibly supportive as I pretty much put life on hold to go down the reader rabbit hole.

Finally, *Strangers to Superfans* is dedicated to Phoenix Sullivan, who taught me everything.

Printed in Great Britain
by Amazon

82116301R00105